LISTENING BEYOND THE ECHOES

Cultural Politics & the Promise of Democracy
A Series from Paradigm Publishers
Edited by Henry A. Giroux

LISTENING BEYOND THE ECHOES
Media, Ethics, and Agency in an Uncertain World

NICK COULDRY

RECEIVED
MAY 3 0 2007
MINNESOTA STATE UNIVERSITY LIBRARY
MANKATO, MN 56002-8419

Paradigm Publishers
Boulder • London

P
94.6
.C687
2006

All rights reserved. No part of this publication may be transmitte   .n any media or form, including electronic, mechanical, photocopy, recc   tional storage and retrieval systems, without the express written consent of the publisher.

Copyright © 2006 by Paradigm Publishers

Published in the United States by Paradigm Publishers, 3360 Mitchell Lane, Suite E, Boulder, Colorado 80301 USA.

Paradigm Publishers is the trade name of Birkenkamp & Company, LLC, Dean Birkenkamp, President and Publisher.

Library of Congress Cataloging-in-Publication Data

Couldry, Nick.
  Listening beyond the echoes : media, ethics, and agency in an uncertain world / Nick Couldry.
      p. cm. — (Cultural politics and the promise of democracy)
  Includes bibliographical references and index.
  ISBN–13: 978–1–59451–235–3 (hc 13)
  ISBN–10: 1–59451–235–3 (hc 10)
  1. Mass media and culture. 2. Mass media—Moral and ethical aspects.
I. Title. II. Cultural politics & the promise of democracy.
  P94.6.C687 2006
  302.23—dc22   2006001593

Printed and bound in the United States of America on acid-free paper that meets the standards of the American National Standard for Permanence of Paper for Printed Library Materials.

Designed and Typeset by Straight Creek Bookmakers.

10   09   08   07   06
1   2   3   4   5

To my friends in Our Media/Nuestros Medios

Contents

-Ͽ

Preface

This book brings together some reflections on the state of media and cultural research at a time of multiple uncertainties—even crises—in democratic engagement, social belonging, the role of universities, the role of media research in the academy, the direction of critical research, and the focus of "the Left."

Most of the book reflects on what in the field of media and cultural research we should be doing in the face of these uncertainties, rather than providing direct analysis of contemporary media. Those who want immediate answers will not therefore be satisfied: my response to their likely complaint is that, with such uncertainties to confront, some reorientation may be necessary, and reorientation means standing still, for a moment, and listening out for new possibilities.

The questions raised by critical media research and cultural analysis are complex; even this book's partial perspective is required to move from media and cultural studies to the social sciences more generally (chapters 2 and 3), across to questions of social exclusion, agency, self-worth, and public connection (chapters 4 and 5), and then to political and democratic theory and questions of ethics and the "good life" (chapters 6 and 7). One chapter—the last—does move beyond reorientation to substantive analysis, but on the new and difficult terrain of media ethics where I have tried to be realistic about how far one author can travel; ethics, is, I believe, vital and neglected in media research, but, to succeed, it requires a collective effort over a long period, to which I hope this book proves a contribution.

Although the context is challenging, the book follows an intuition that the necessary reorientation involves foregrounding quite simple questions:

What practices of daily life are media involved in? How do media contribute to the "culture" of democratic politics? How can we live, ethically, with and through media?

Even so, the book's emphasis on second-order questions may still strike some as strange. In global circumstances of considerable conflict and danger, shouldn't all our energies be devoted, for example, to deconstructing the ideological discourse of the current U.S. and UK administrations or the growing corporate monopolization of media industries? Of course, that's important, but there are other ways of responding to the dangers of our time. If we suspect that media—that is, highly centralized institutional processes of mediation—are integral, not incidental, to the current crisis of Western democracy, and if we suspect also that one path beyond that crisis lies in listening very carefully to how citizens are experiencing the consequences of that crisis for their own sense of agency, then "direct" research into media texts and institutions needs to be supplemented by other (as I will call them) decentered strategies for understanding mediated societies. And the most important response of all to the current crises may be to try and develop, in terms that escape the pull of media discourse, a framework for assessing whether media's contribution to our collective and individual lives is as we want and need it to be.

Earlier versions of chapters 3 and 5 under the same titles were published in Social Semiotics (vol. 14[2]: 115–132, 2004) and The Review of Education, Pedagogy and Cultural Studies (vol. 26[1]: 3–21, 2004). Thanks to Taylor & Francis (UK) and Taylor & Francis Group LLC, respectively, for permission to republish materials from those articles; the original versions are viewable via each journal's website (respectively, www.tandf.co.uk and www.taylorandfrancis.com). Chapter 6 contains material previously published as "Beyond the televised endgame? Addressing the long-term consequences of global media inequality," in N. Chitty, R. Rush, and M. Semati (eds.), Studies in Terrorism: Media Scholarship and the Enigma of Terror, Penang: Southbound Press, 2003: thanks to Southbound Press for permission to republish this material.

I owe a great debt to Henry Giroux for suggesting the possibility of this book and for comments on the whole manuscript that saved me from a number of confusions; and an equally great debt to Dean Birkenkamp for being an extremely supportive and responsive publisher. Thanks to James Curran and Roger Silverstone for helpful comments on a much earlier draft of chapter 7. Needless to say, responsibility for the remaining errors is mine.

Thanks also to my colleagues in the Department of Media and Communications at the London School of Economics for providing a very stimulating environment over the last four years in which to get this work done.

Heartfelt thanks to my wife, Louise Edwards, for her patience, support, and love, without which this book could not have been written.

I dedicate this book to my friends in the Our Media/Nuestros Medios network, whose work contests on a daily basis many of the injustices that, more indirectly, I address here. I could not wish for more inspiring collaborators in the wider world of media and cultural research than they.

That is why I take as the start of the book a quotation from a work of community-based media, the Enciclopedia Cultural de Chiloé, published in many volumes by the Fundacion Radio Estrella del Mar, from the Chiloé region of Chile (for background, see Rodriguez, 2003). The quotation is from its preface, written by Bishop Ysern, one of the work's main inspirations and facilitators. Thanks to Angelica Rosas and Soledad Lorca from Radio Estrella del Mar who attended the Our Media/ Nuestros Medios III conference in Barranquilla, Colombia, in May 2003 and generously gave me a copy of this remarkable work.

Nick Couldry
August 2005

Es necesario que se oigan todas las voces en el concierto de la vida.
It is necessary that all voices are heard in the concert of life.
—Bishop Juan Luis Ysern de Arce

1
Introduction: Listening Out for Connections

✧

> I wanted to make a sociology that will look back and talk back. ... [It is]
> the project of creating a way of seeing, from where we actually live, into the
> powers, processes, and relations that organize and determine the everyday
> life context of that seeing.
>
> —Dorothy Smith

In these words, Dorothy Smith, the Canadian feminist sociologist (1987:
8–9), expressed as well as anyone the point of a critical sociology: to look
back at, to talk back to, structures of power that are deeply embedded in
the contexts and forms of our daily life. But one term is missing, although
perhaps implicit: to *listen*. Listening out for new forms of critical connection
is the point of this book.

In introducing an aural metaphor, I do not want to suggest that sound
should be privileged over sight, even though the dominance of the visual
in Western modernity has often been noted (Levin, 1989). This book's title
is instead an attempt to characterize a way of addressing the density of the
contemporary, media-saturated world that does not, necessarily, accept it
on its own terms (generally characterized visually). I want in these chapters
to develop a way of responding to media saturation that does not look *back*
to the stream of media images and signals, but instead listens *out* for wider
patterns and disruptions.

Grasping the significance of media in the contemporary world is like
trying to assess the speed and noise of daily life by standing in the mouth

of a motorway tunnel. While there may be other realities a short walk away, none can rival the incessant rush of oncoming traffic for the person standing close by. So too with the daily stream of media: often it seems to be the main reality with which we must engage (cf. Gitlin, 2001), and yet we know that it takes just a short journey to find a site from where we might reflect critically on whether media are the main reality to which we must attend. There is an issue, then, of where we need to stand to get the best vantage point on media's contributions (good and bad) to contemporary life.

How is the tradition of critical research on media and popular culture in the United States, United Kingdom, and elsewhere placed on this issue? There is no doubting the importance of this tradition, stretching back more than four decades and given various overlapping and contested names (communication research, media studies, cultural studies); without its empirical sensitivity and theoretical sophistication, our understanding of media institutions and representational practices and, more fundamentally, the ways people live with, and around, media would be poor indeed. Yet from the beginning, such research has been on the defensive. Against those academics (still far too many) who would like to block their ears, it has insisted that we must understand how media work and the role they play in people's lives: ignoring the motorway tunnel is no answer! But the historic success of this strategy since the 1970s in establishing a position within the academy for media and cultural research, even if an embattled one, is no guarantee of its usefulness for the future.

Key to media research's strategy to date has been a critical focus on the main dimensions of media as product: the media text, the institutions that produce it, and (from the 1980s onward) the audiences that interpret it. Central to the tradition of cultural studies has been the argument that culture and particularly popular culture must be taken seriously as a site of meaning, creativity, agency, and identity. At first glance, it is not obvious why these strategies should change. However, not only are both traditions mature enough now to review where they are heading, but also these are challenging times: times of democratic disengagement, state and corporate lies on a huge scale, increasing poverty even in the most developed countries, and the impoverishment of political discourse by spectacle.

What if now we need to imagine different strategies for media and cultural research, a different formulation of our priorities and purpose? This is the possibility the book explores.

What if, to grasp better how media work with and against particular ways of organizing social and private life, we need to move across the landscape: looking at the buildings and fields beside the motorway as it emerges from the tunnel; walking along the routes connected by the motorway but also, of course, connectable by other routes; noting the byways *not* linked directly to the motorway system at all—before returning to the sites alongside the tunnel that the motorway displaced? If we are to understand how media work in contemporary societies, we must also know how to walk—slowly, attentively, with our ears open and not blocked—*away* from the roar of the traffic. That way we may be able to hear different connections—provided, of course, our ears aren't so worn down that we hear only repetitions of the traffic's din.

If the resources to tell stories and have others listen to them are, in contemporary societies, highly concentrated and if media institutions benefit from a large proportion of that concentration (undeniable, however interactive media formats become), then the *symbolic power* (as we might call it) of media institutions is surely a major theme for critical sociology, that is, a sociology that cares about analyzing power.[1] Indeed, a large part of media research over the past half century has addressed aspects of this issue, or at least its consequences for social representations, if often with surprisingly little recognition from mainstream sociology. This book is an attempt—inevitably from the partial perspective of one writer—to review how the elements of that critical strategy now hold together as a model for the future: both a model of future research and, through that, a possible framework for public debate about the differences (good and bad) that media make to the world. This introductory chapter aims to give an advance map of the terrain we cover, while at the same time asking why these questions are so difficult, and why resistance to confronting them should be so great.

False or Missing Trails

The fallacy, sadly, of much postmodern reflection on media from Baudrillard onward, for all its insights, is to mistake the damage media's incessant messages have done to its hearing for a nuanced understanding of media's actual workings in the social world. Media work in ways more complex, uneven, and open to challenge than postmodernist theory allows.

Take the example of terrorism. This is a dimension of today's mediated world that postmodernism appeared to have encompassed in advance (Baudrillard, 1983). But we can see now, particularly after 9/11, which was in part an attack on a city, New York, that represented one of the world's largest concentrations of symbolic power, how Baudrillard was wrong in his earlier reading of terrorist attacks as "hyperreal events, no longer having any particular contents or aims, but indefinitely refracted by each other" (1983: 41). This misinterpretation stemmed from forgetting that the inequality in the conditions of symbolic production that underlies the mediated surface

3

of world events remains *real*, not hyperreal, and hence something it is meaningful to contest *as such*. Postmodernism's philosophically driven readings of the media's social consequences are blind to the real unevennesses in how the benefits and costs of media's particular disposition of symbolic resources differentially affect individuals, groups, classes, countries, and even religions. This is why postmodernism mistakes terrorism for a dispute within the discourse of the sign, when in part it is a contest about the authority of the sign, and about the material conditions of its production (cf. chapter 6).

By contrast, other social thought gives us only a rather blurred tracking of media's social significance. Take this startling image: "The goal of sociological analysis must now be to discover what freedom, solidarity, and equality might mean in a social situation in which the centre ... is empty, and in which the throne room is full of draughts and has been invaded by bands of speculators and paparazzi" (Touraine, 2000: 11).

Here, toward the beginning of his book *Can We Live Together?* the French sociologist Alain Touraine provokes us to think about the complex ways in which our times are out of joint. The image of the paparazzi in the throne room startles because their presence seems so obviously illegitimate. But who or what are the paparazzi photographing? Is it just the chaos left by a fading political regime? Is it the tired figures of Western democracy's old ideals that Touraine argues we must move beyond? Or is it the celebrities who, as Touraine's image at least implies, have been installed in the throne room instead of the old royal family?

This blurring in Touraine's otherwise brilliant image is perhaps symptomatic of a more general blurring in how social and political thought addresses media: the media are there, their trace caught inevitably in our image of what is happening to the social world, but the figure is blurred. So questions of what exactly media do, and why they matter, go partly unanswered, even unformulated.

If we put postmodernism-influenced sociology to one side, some sociological thought does acknowledge the importance of media and has done so for three decades (Giddens, 1975). But a difficulty—perhaps one reason for the blurring we see in Touraine's image—is that media span both the most general and the highly particular. Media are, in a sense, everywhere, and yet wherever we look, the substance of media and how they work is highly particular: *this* image, *this* news story, *this* interview. Media are a pervasive, highly regular, reliably structured process for representing the social world both in its particularities and its generality, a process that never stops although it often claims finality and definitiveness for itself. It is extremely difficult therefore to isolate any particular consequence of media—the classic problem of media effects whose implications are discussed in chapters 2 and 3. As a result, it has often been easier to ignore media than to consider how far media compel the rethinking of elements of social analysis.

Sometimes there is a good alibi: the edifice of classical thinking about democracy and ethics evolved well before the full emergence of modern media institutions. Media don't integrate well into either political theory or ethics because, historically, they were not intended to. As a result, while the consequences of mediated access to the political process should be a central consideration within political theory, they are surprisingly marginal. The absence of media ethics as a reference point in the negotiations of everyday life is also surprising, and perhaps more suspicious. We at least know where to begin in challenging the unauthorized intrusion of a policeman or doctor or social worker into our private lives, but who knows how to challenge media representatives when they seek to intervene in our lives? There is, of course, much generalized popular scepticism, even hostility, toward what media do, for example, in relation to hounded celebrities. But that scepticism is not the same as a developed ethical framework for deciding what citizens in a democracy *should do* about media. Perhaps this absence has something to do with the influence of media institutions over what is articulated *as* the contestable issues within everyday life.

And yet the pervasive presence of media raises specific issues for understanding power in relation to politics or ethics that we cannot ignore. In the case of politics, particularly as fears for the health of democratic engagement grow in the United States and the United Kingdom, we must ask What is the contribution of people's media consumption to their possibilities of being political agents? There is a wider link here to cultural studies' theme (from Raymond Williams onward) of the search for a common culture and the promise of democracy (explored further in chapters 4 and 5).

In relation to media ethics, problematic cases are easy to come by, even if articulating their wider implications is difficult. A vivid example comes from the film *City of God* (director Fernando Meirelles, 2002) about conditions in a *favela* of Rio de Janeiro. The only way out of the *favela* for any character in the film is when a young man takes photographic images that get used in the Rio newspapers, bringing glamour to the *favela's* gang leaders and exposing gangland violence to ultimately corrupt police intervention. In the end nothing is resolved by the circulation of these images, except that the photographer narrator finds a way out of the *favela,* and so the film's story comes to be told. But what of the power issues raised by the taking of those images, and what of the ethical implications of this process? The film doesn't raise them, and they are not easy to formulate—typical, perhaps, of the uncertain area of media ethics. From which standpoint can we offer such a formulation? This is not obvious, and in chapter 7 we will have to do a great deal of work to build even the starting points for a framework of media ethics.

Listening Out

Where to go from here? If media are a problematic object for social science to register—both enormously pervasive and highly particular—then maybe "picturing" media neatly in the social terrain is doomed to failure. We need another way of thinking about how to register media's social presence. And here perhaps a shift of the sense of perception that dominates our metaphors may help.

If media are something like an environment or "ecology" in contemporary societies (Chaney, 2002: 53),[2] then we cannot, and should not, separate out the issues of factual analysis from the issues of ethics. Indeed, in thinking about the media environment, analysis and evaluation are inseparable: We study and analyze media from a place *within* the media environment, so we cannot *not* care about that environment's consequences for us and for others.

This sense that what we do as researchers is embedded in the very process we are studying is captured better by aural than by visual metaphors; as John Dewey put it, "vision is a spectator; hearing is a participator" (Dewey, 1946: 219). David Michael Levin (1989) has done much to bring out the distinctive features of the sense of hearing and therefore to suggest its advantages as a source of metaphors for thinking about the social world. Key in his account are the reciprocal, embodied nature of listening, its embeddedness always in an intersubjective space of perception. This captures exactly the point I wish to suggest: that how we deal, as researchers and as individuals, with media is not a remote question, but integral to the quality of contemporary life—hence it embraces all aspects of theory and analysis up to and including ethics.

It is striking that one of the sharpest and oldest questions asked about media's social consequences was formulated in aural terms. Written in 1936, Walter Benjamin's essay "The Storyteller" examines the decline in storytelling and its implications for the "communicability of experience" (1968: 93). Although aspects of Benjamin's argument have little to do with media (his reflections on the consequences for returning soldiers of the horrors of World War I), part of it remains relevant to and controversial within media research.[3] Benjamin suggests that stories have increasingly been replaced with *information*—facts that come with an explanatory context (or at least the assumption of one) but are at the same time detached from the less definitive presence of the human storyteller: "No event any longer comes to us without already being shot through with explanation. In other words, by now almost nothing that happens benefits storytelling; almost everything benefits information" (1972: 89).

Benjamin implies that storytelling is more and more detached from the human qualities of the storyteller and therefore that the ethical questions that would automatically arise with a story become increasingly difficult to attach to the social flow of information. If in the early twenty-first century we repeat Benjamin's question—stories or information?—we surely recognize its salience; most of us drown in often unwanted information, yet the search for an ethics of information, and media, remains unsatisfied.

This book cannot hope to provide definite answers to this or other large questions about media's consequences for the social world. Its aim is more preliminary: to lay the foundations of a framework within which answers could be generated in the future. For any chance of formulating better answers requires distance. We need to listen beyond the echoes of the media process and search for new starting points for critical engagement within everyday practice. Once again, it is worth explaining that my choice of an aural metaphor to link the book's chapters does *not* mean claiming that the aural is somehow superior to the visual. Such either/or thinking is unhelpful, since both aural and visual responses to media are, of course, crucial. The aim, simply, is to offer an organizing metaphor for an *alternative* perspective on the overwhelming presence of media in our lives, an alternative perspective that I believe is much needed.

All the chapters in this book, then, search in different ways for a perspective outside the media process from which to grasp its wider significance. Chapters 2 and 3 address this in relation to media analysis specifically; chapters 4 and 5 range more widely to questions of culture and agency, particularly political agency, in an attempt to rethink the direction of cultural studies. Chapters 6 and 7 open out the difficult question of media ethics in terms that address, potentially, a global, and not just a local or national, scale.

Yet—and this is worth emphasizing—for all its critical stance toward media and media culture, this book is not antipopular. Rather it attempts to reconnect with everyday practice oriented toward media and listen to the complex mix of engagement *and* disengagement, enjoyment *and* distaste, that characterizes many people's reflexive relationship to media.

There is, as Hanno Hardt (2005) has recently noted, a critical tradition of media analysis from Latin America (see especially Martin-Barbero, 1993) that recognizes media's possible overlaps with popular forms of pleasure, literacy, and political resistance but that makes no easy assumptions that the product of a highly centralized, usually commercialized system of cultural transmission is necessarily popular or progressive. This tradition sees the media process as never separable from questions of power, where by *power* we mean not just military, economic, or political power, but "the actual authority of those in control of the means of communication ... the ... ability to influence the construction of fact or fiction" (Hardt, 2005: 101). This is the power inherent to the process of mediation (cf. Carey, 1989; Curran, 2002)—symbolic power or, as Bourdieu once put it, "the power of constructing reality" (1990: 166). There is no adequate way of thinking about what media and popular culture mean without also thinking about their embedding in relations of power, above all, the power inherent in the possibility of their being expressed at all. Value and politics, agency and ethics must be thought together.

Hardt's reflections return us to the purpose of critical social research, this time specifically media research: "Reading the relations between communication and power provides a contemporary measure of the condition of democracy and the limits of communication itself" (Hardt, 2005: 105–106). This makes clear that to seek a space beyond the immediate imperatives and rhetoric of the media process is not to be antimedia. It is to take seriously media's claims to contribute to the texture of the social world and the health of democratic politics, but in no way to take the truth of those claims as given. The importance of media institutions' potential to call states to account can, of course, only increase, not decrease, in an era of heightened militarism and corporate theft committed or encouraged by those with political responsibility.

We need, then, media and cultural research that is critical, ethically reflexive, and ready to track media's consequences across the breadth of everyday life; we should not be afraid to take a fresh look at our priorities in researching media and culture, and how these fit into the wider terrain of social science. Exploring these questions is the task of this book.

Notes

1. Cf. Wright Mills (1970) [1959]; Alvin Gouldner (1962).
2. See also Mueller (2004) for an interesting policy-focused argument on the parallels between media reform and the environmental movement.
3. For a critical development of his argument in relation to contemporary media, see Scannell (1988).

PART I
Media, Social "Order," Agency

2
Decentering Media Research
Social "Order," Knowledge, and Agency

᪐

It seems simple: the focus of media research is *media,* in the term's usual double usage, media texts and the institutions that produce those texts. Certainly, while media texts and institutions were ignored by traditional academic disciplines, things *were* that simple. A great deal of the achievements of media and communication research in the 1970s and 1980s consisted in showing, in great detail, why media (in both senses) mattered as a social reference point; as a reproducer of ideology; as an economic force, and, of course, as a source of pleasure, information, and mystification in people's daily lives. These achievements of media studies (from the analysis of news discourse to the political economy of media to the important extension of audience research) will not disappear and will no doubt continue to be developed.

With such a record of success, there must be a strong argument for conservatism when it comes to thinking about the future agenda of media research; as the saying goes, "If it ain't broke, don't fix it." That, I suggest, would be a mistake. There are risks, as always, in trying to stay fixed while many parameters outside one's control are changing (and the whole media landscape is certainly undergoing change, whether in terms of genre, or multimedia platforms, or online/mobile delivery, or global market concentrations). It would also be a mistake to believe that media research has achieved all there is to achieve. For that would ignore something rather embarrassing: media research remains quite marginal in academic hierarchies and reference points, when compared to sociology, anthropology, or economics. How much has media *research* shifted the agendas of those disciplines? Very little, I suspect, even if media themselves have, of course, been addressed by them to varying degrees.

There may be some rather uninteresting prejudices behind this situation, but there is also, I suggest, a more substantive reason for media research's continued marginality: a genuine disagreement between it and those traditional disciplines about how central media actually are to the explanation of contemporary change. Sometimes this crystallizes in a charge of *mediacentrism;* an early example would be the late 1970s debate over the "dominant ideology thesis" when certain non-Marxist critics challenged how important ideology (including media-circulated ideology) actually was in sustaining capitalism, compared with economic forces (Abercrombie et al., 1981); more often, the issue is left implicit in accounts of contemporary society that say very little directly about media. Far from *defending* media studies against the implied charge of mediacentrism, I want to suggest the charge is partly *right;* indeed, acknowledging that it is right may in the long run be the best way of media studies' becoming less isolated from other social science disciplines and thereby establishing itself more securely in the disciplinary terrain. But this is where things become less simple.

Whatever the possible strategic advantage of accepting that media studies' mediacentrism is wrong, the move can be made only if this admission allows us to see *more* clearly what the real object of media research is, which requires, inevitably, a more complex account of that object than just "media." At the very least, this means defining the object of media studies as the consequences of media for the social world.[1] But if our aim is to understand as clearly as possible the *consequences* of media for the social world, then it cannot be valid to assume in advance what we want to find out: so it must be wrong (and this is why mediacentrism is a fallacy) to *assume* that media are more consequential than other institutions that structure the social world (economic, material, spatial, and so on). And this means acknowledging that sometimes, perhaps more often than as media researchers we suspect, media are *less* consequential in the social world than other forces (such as changes in the labor market or in family structure). Equally, since causality in the social sciences is rarely a simple matter of either/or, it means acknowledging that the media dimensions of a cultural phenomenon may be less important than other dimensions—or at least allowing for this possibility until we can show to others' satisfaction outside media research exactly how those media dimensions take effect.

Because any academic discipline needs some working assumptions to get anything done and because, as already noted, the assumption that media research is about media (plain and simple) has served media research very well till now, I realize that opening up such questions may cause discomfort in some quarters. What I hope to show, however, over the next two chapters is that a *decentered* media studies—that is, media research whose assumptions and priorities are media-*oriented*, but not media-*centered*—raises new and interesting questions, questions that bring media research closer to the problematics of other social sciences, without sacrificing any of media research's historic achievements.

More than that, a decentered media studies is fun, because it allows us to ask questions and follow up leads that previously might have seemed illegitimate. It is also politically more agile, since it enables us as media researchers to maintain a safe distance from media institutions' own claims for their significance and legitimacy (and political forces' reliance on those claims to further their own ends).

I will discuss the decentering of media research in two stages, separating mediacentrism from the related but distinct set of assumptions that elsewhere I have called "the myth of the mediated center" (Couldry, 2003a). Once this deconstructive work is out of the way, we will be able to explore two more positive themes: first, some interesting, if difficult, theoretical questions about media's contribution to social "order"; and, second, what happens to the agenda of media research after we have "decentered" it.

What's Wrong with Mediacentrism?

One of the first media researchers to argue explicitly against mediacentrism was the Colombian media theorist Jesus Martin-Barbero (1993). That he was Latin American is probably no accident, since modern media arrived late in many Latin American countries (in Brazil, for example, television was a national force only from the 1970s with improved satellite transmission, and, because of transportation costs, the press was not the early force it was in other countries; see Mattelart and Mattelart, 1990); in any case, modern media came centuries after the historical trauma of the colonial conquest and subsequent expulsions of colonial forces. A merely mediacentric account of popular culture in Latin America would be absurd, even though Latin America has generated media forms (notably the *telenovela*) of astonishing audience reach.

The issue of mediacentrism was, however, implicitly raised when UK audience research turned toward the study of everyday life in the late 1980s and early 1990s (Silverstone, 1994). This work looked very carefully at the conditions under which to varying degrees information and communication technologies such as television and computers were *domesticated*, that is, inserted into lasting positions within everyday routines; here media, as objects and as access points in systems of information circulation, took their place alongside other domestic technologies such as central heating systems and the car (Silverstone and Hirsch, 1992), not to mention the dynamics of family life, education, and so on. In chapter 3, I argue that we can see this version of audience studies—which heavily privileged the technological dimensions of media over media as text—as part of an interrupted history of decentered media research that we might now resume in the course of retheorizing media as "practice."

There are no doubt other episodes in the history of media research that we could take as forerunners of a decentered approach. But there are very many others that face in the opposite direction, or at least fail to raise explicitly the question of how the processes they describe (within media texts or media institutions or audiences) are *consequential* for the wider social terrain.

It would be unfair to put the blame all one way. For we can also find signs of the opposite assumption in other disciplines: the fallacy, if you like, of *media marginalism*. I am no longer surprised when I pick up a book on, say, social theory or social power and, looking in the index, find no references to media. The idea that media institutions and media texts are completely *in*consequential in the social world is as strange, perhaps even stranger, than the idea of mediacentrism. So, in reading both sociology and media research, one may sometimes get the impression of a dialogue of the deaf (without sign language): mediacentrism meets media marginalism.

Perhaps there is a deeper problem here. Consider this quote from an extremely sophisticated and exhaustive investigation into the sociology of the individual: "[There is] a complexification of social situations which are less overhung [*surplombées*] by textual universes imposed by the media or other means of mass communications than structured verbally with the help of pieces of various narratives circulating between different social positions" (Martuccelli, 2002: 360–361).

"Imposed by the media?" Even the term *overhung* suggests a threat from a distant source. This is a surprisingly throwaway comment on the possible relevance of media languages in the course of a book-length analysis of the various social bases that sustain the "individual" in advanced capitalist societies. There is no sense here that media might be integral to the texture of at least some people's lives and, indeed, might be one of the supports of individualization that we need to theorize. A similar disinterest in media's intimate role in people's lives is found in Bourdieu et al.'s large book of interviews on "social suffering," *The Weight of the World* (1999; for discussion, see Couldry, 2005b). Other sociologists (Giddens, 1991; Beck, 1992) have been more responsive to the significance of media, for example, in circulating new forms of identity narration or new reference points for political or cultural allegiance, but even here it is fair to say that neither Beck nor Giddens spends much time on the detail of how media flows have the consequences they do.

We start to get a sense of what the problem might be when we look at the work of a sociologist who is very sympathetic to the media's importance in cultural explanation and, indeed, has pioneered this within mainstream sociology—David Chaney (1994). Chaney's recent book (2002) attempts some bold theorizations of how media alter social organization: take his notion of the "informalization" of contemporary culture (2002: chapter 5) and his interesting discussion of how the "extraordinary" world of media can be reworked within the "ordinary" dimensions of media and everyday life (2002: chapter 6). The problem, however, is that any *detailed* causal mechanism for explaining how these media influences might work or, indeed, what exact shape those influences might take is missing from Chaney's account.

So the problem—and the underlying explanation for both unjustified mediacentrism and unargued media marginalism—may be the sheer *difficulty* of accounting for how media flows, whether particular segments, or the whole flow, or aspects of it have consequences in the social world. As forty years of media research have shown from many directions (from Cultivation Theory debates to audience research to discourse analysis), this is a very tricky problem that remains in part unanswered. Little wonder, then, that sociologists often find it easier to ignore media "effects" altogether, and media researchers often find it easier simply to assume the priority of media factors (they are unlikely to use the term *media effects* since we know better than that media research!). The result is that a potentially interesting debate between sociology and media research about how to think through, on both micro and macro levels, the *mechanisms* by which media messages are embedded in social action has not really begun.

I put things this way, not to raise hopes that this book can solve the problem—it cannot—but simply to suggest that a good start toward that dialogue with the wider social sciences is for media researchers to drop any vestiges of mediacentrism from our language and thereby *open up* the difficult causal questions about how and to what extent media *materials* work in the social world.

The Myth of the Mediated Center

We face, however, another obstacle to decentering media research—in the sense of abandoning the assumption of mediacentrism, but not, of course, our orientation toward questions about media—and this comes from a misreading of media's causal consequences whose origins lie well beyond academic research, even if it is quite easy for media studies to be caught up in it. I mean the discourse that in previous writings I have labeled "the myth of the mediated center" (Couldry 2003a: chapter 3).

This is the social construction of centralized media (*the media* in common parlance) as our privileged access point to the *central realities* of the social world, whatever they are. This myth builds on an underlying myth that society has a center. Let me explain.

It might seem strange to say that the idea of a social center is mythical. Surely, all large complex societies *do* have a center: a center of government, the state, that manages certain key dimensions of social organization (the economy, taxation, education, military defense, and public order—let's leave aside the details of how those areas are divided up between federal and state/regional powers in different countries); that governmental center is associated with a head of state who may or may not be a member of the government but either way has the role of representing the state and society on ceremonial occasions. Surely this *is* a center—and remember, we haven't even begun to list all the more subtle ways in which contemporary governments exercise regulatory and other powers that influence behavior within their territory.

All this is obviously true, and I would not deny it for a moment. What I mean by the myth of the center, however, is the idea that this *organizational* center, which will always in practice be complex (that is, the site of multiple, competing forces: political, economic, social, cultural), is also a center of *social values and coherence.*[2]

Again, one might argue that the state *is* involved in orchestrating social values and narratives about what is going on in societies; in this sense, surely, we cannot neglect the state's role in providing such explanatory coherence as contemporary societies have. The concession made here is crucial: "such explanatory coherence as contemporary societies have." For there is here an assumption (of coherence, linked to underlying values and social order) that needs to be empirically investigated, not *assumed.* It is this uncertainty that the metaphor of social center (in the sense of a center of value and coherence) obscures. Worse, by encouraging us to take for granted the notion that society has an explanatory center that *contains* its core values, the myth of the center invites us to assume what we should definitely not assume: that social values are generated by that center. Even worse, the myth of the center (unless, that is, we grasp it as a myth) encourages us to see order and coherence in the social terrain where, if we looked differently, we might see disorder or a lesser degree of order: disputes over value, contests over legitimacy, alternative explanations of social change to those that give primacy to a social center.

The myth of the center is at the root of a fundamental mistake long ago identified in the social sciences: functionalism. This is the idea that society is a functioning whole whose parts each contribute to the better operation, or "functioning," of the whole. This idea, though it has a long history, depends quite clearly on a metaphor: seeing society as a body or machine, a self-sufficient, self-adjusting entity.[3] But it is a huge leap to see a complex society in these terms, whatever the *pressures toward* order that undoubtedly exist within it.

Instead, we should look sceptically at whether contemporary mediated societies actually *do* hold together (cf. Lukes, 1975), with the help of media or otherwise. The very idea of *the social*, which is assumed, for example, behind notions that rituals integrate societies, is the result of a constant production (Hall, 1977: 340); so too is our sense that in certain places and times we come together as a society through, for example, media. This is not to dismiss as insignificant the rhetorical claims that are frequently made by various institutions about society, the nation, the people; but it does mean rethinking their significance as precisely *rhetorical*, not taking them at face value. As the Israeli anthropologist Don Handelman has explained, any social network will tend to have "media through which members communicate to themselves in concert about the characters of their collectivities, *as if* these do constitute entities that are temporarily coherent. Public events are convergences of this kind" (Handelman, 1998: 15). In contemporary societies dominated by highly concentrated media forms, the rhetorical pressures to believe in such convergences are very great.

In other words, in contemporary societies, the myth of the center (with all of its functionalist baggage) is inseparable from the myth of the *mediated* center: the myth that media institutions are our privileged, or central, access point to the social center. Within this second myth, too, a crucial fact is given an aura of naturalness: yes, media comprise one of the crucial centralizations of resources in society, in this case, the centralization of symbolic resources, and media therefore have a close link with the other forms of resource centralization we have been discussing. But, once again, that does not mean media are a center of social value or coherence. Nor must we fall into the trap, in thinking about media, of assuming that behind the media's workings there lies the social center, for that would be to allow functionalism in through the back door.

Elsewhere I've discussed in detail the impact of the myth of the mediated center in media research (Couldry, 2005a) and the need to move beyond it. It is important to see, however, that the myth of the mediated center is not just, and not even primarily, a confusion of academic thinking. It is a pervasive feature of media discourse: media, after all, are consistently *telling* us (whether explicitly or implicitly) that they speak for us, express our values; sometimes this is in opposition to what the state appears to want (when governments are challenged), other times not (when we are summoned to war).

This, then, is one important difference between mediacentrism and the myth of the mediated center: the former is a bias in academic argument that makes unjustified assumptions about the relative importance of media (after all, there are also the economy, family life, spatial organization, and so on, to consider). The myth of the mediated center, by contrast, is a naturalized pattern of discourse that may be reproduced in media research but can crop up anywhere, including in media's own accounts of their importance in the world. Mediacentrism misleads us about the relative importance of a particular causal factor (media) in explaining social processes; the myth of the mediated center misleads us, more fundamentally, about what is "there" to be explained in the social sciences, the very idea that there is a social center at all. (So we might say mediacentrism is an epistemological error, whereas the myth of the mediated center is an ontological error.)

It follows that it is quite possible to make one error without the other. We could deconstruct fully the myth of the mediated center (e.g., within a postmodern sceptical account about whether the social world holds together), and yet make unwarranted assumptions about media's relative importance in social explanation; in fact, many postmodern accounts of media saturation do precisely this! Equally, we could give media a relatively modest role in fundamental social explanation, but nonetheless, when referring to media, to treat them as standing in for a broader social center (as, for example, certain types of functionalism are ready to do). Worse, the epistemological error can easily become associated with the more fundamental, ontological one: if we are insufficiently cautious about assessing the high causal priority we give to media, then it may easily happen that we give too much credence to media's often inflated discourse about itself and its significance for society or the nation; in doing the latter, we may find ourselves adopting a functionalism through the back door. This is perhaps why, against the grain of media studies' wider theoretical sophistication, functionalism has gained a surprising hold here, even though it has long been expelled from sociology and anthropology.

So there are additional stakes—both theoretical and political—in avoiding both mediacentrism and the myth of the mediated center; they are major benefits of a decentered media research. Let me briefly discuss both aspects, starting with the political.

The Political Stakes

I start with politics since it flows directly from our consideration of the myth of the mediated center, although it arises also, but more subtly, in relation to mediacentrism.

A decentered media research—which openly considers the *varying* importance that media, among the whole range of causal factors, may have in society—reduces, although it cannot entirely remove, the risk of our assuming that the sites where most resources are concentrated (the state and, in the case of symbolic resources, the media) are also both value-center and the starting-point of social explanation. It should make us more sceptical also about *whether* a social center in this sense exists at all.

This is politically important, I suggest, when, at the risk of oversimplifying processes that inevitably are more complex in their detail:

1. Certain states, particularly the United States and United Kingdom, are pursuing linked military and economic policies (militarily enhanced neoliberalism) about which large numbers of their own populations, let alone the rest of the world, have grave reservations;
2. Those states have considerable resources to orchestrate media spectacles and other ritualized events that further legitimate their power and strategies.

From the first point, it follows (and few would disagree) that critical research needs a distance from the discourses that legitimate those states' actions. From the second point, it follows, perhaps more controversially, that critical research—above all critical media research—needs maximum distance from the *mediated* discourse through which those states' legitimacy is sustained.

This is not to suggest, of course, that media discourses, whether in the United States, United Kingdom, or elsewhere, are simply compliant with state strategies; in the United Kingdom at least, opposition to UK involvement in the U.S. invasion of Iraq has run right through media institutions, as well as through the civil and diplomatic services, the armed forces, and civil society. But it is to suggest that we need our critical distance from both media and state discourses since the potential implication of the former in the latter is subtle.

The long-running misconception in U.S. public opinion about the alleged link between Iraq and the September 11 attacks is perhaps a clear enough justification for such distance. In the United Kingdom, as I wrote just a month or so after the week that combined the terrible London bombings of July 7, 2005, Britain's success in its bid to stage the 2012 Olympics, and the Live8 concert preceding the G-8 Gleneagles Summit, the importance of critical distance from media discourse needs more explaining. Let me concentrate on the issue of interpreting politics, although there are many other aspects of contemporary culture (e.g., celebrity culture) where a decentered media research has benefit.

It is surely striking to find across the political scale from left to right the same ideological closure in praise of the prime minister's charismatic powers during the week of those events (d'Ancona, 2005; Kettle, 2005). The language of the *Guardian*'s left-of-center commentator is, not surprisingly given Tony Blair's controversial status on the left, more cautious in making explicit references to charisma:

> Blair has a future and not just a past ... The winning of the Olympics [bid] may not be on a par with Europe [Blair's June 2004 speech to the European Parliament] and the G-8 agenda, but his role and his commitment—echoes of the effort he put into the Northern Ireland peace talks [in 1998]—were nevertheless remarkable ... Intense personal effort, again as part of a team, played a huge part in making Gleneagles a much more substantial event than the usual forgettable summit get-together ... I accept that when some people see Blair in such settings they see a war criminal or a congenital liar. But those who respond that way should accept that many more people round the planet see someone else; the leading and most articulate statesman in the developed world. (Kettle, 2005)

Matthew d'Ancona in the conservative *Sunday Telegraph* was less cautious in his language:

> As I watched the Prime Minister being helicoptered back and forth from Gleneagles, I was reminded again of Blair Mark One, who, through sleepnessness and sheer force of character, coaxed the parties in Ulster into signing the Good Friday Agreement in 1998. Did the deal hold together? Of course not. But it was still an extraordinary feat of leadership, a dramatisation of what was *possible* in Northern Ireland: its form was, so to speak, its content.... I choose my words with care. As I say, Mr Blair is a remarkable statesman.... In no week since he first entered Downing Street has it been more obvious why he has for so long dominated the political landscape of a country that in seven extraordinary days ran the full gamut of emotions and did not find its Prime Minister wanting. (d'Ancona, 2005)

The reference to charisma in d'Ancona's final sentence is clear; we know enough about charismatic power (Weber, 1991a) to keep an analytic distance from it. But notice another phrase: "Its form was, so to speak, its content." We might agree, perhaps, that the symbolism of the 1998 Northern Ireland peace talks was crucial, but to value form over content as a general principle? This is all too convenient a stance when the content of government policy is so problematic. The (necessary) blindness to the problems of policy content by current U.S.–UK policymakers was expressed powerfully by Gary Younge in a rare article dissenting from the media consensus in the immediate aftermath of the bombings:

It is no mystery why those who have backed the war in Iraq would refute this con-nection [between the London bombings and the Iraq invasion]. With each and every setback, from the lack of UN endorsement right through to the continuing strength of the insurgency, they go ever deeper into denial. Their sophistry has now mutated into a form of political autism—their ability to engage with the world around them has been severely impaired by their adherence to a flawed and fatal project. (Younge, 2005)

The difference between the dominant media consensus in Britain about Blair in early July 2005 and this rare public voice of dissent could hardly be sharper: form versus content, admiration for personal charisma versus attention to the fundamental contradictions between a "statesman's" fine words and his vicariously violent actions (Blair is the most belliger-ent UK prime minister of recent decades). Perhaps the reality of a war justified by deceit is too difficult to keep in focus. Paul Krugman, com-menting on the parallel gap between rhetoric and reality in the U.S. government's selling of the Iraq war goes further: "[This] is arguably the worst scandal in American political history.... Indeed the idea that we were deceived into war makes many commentators so uncomfortable that they refuse to admit the possibility" (Krugman 2004, quoted in Giroux, forthcoming, b).

We need, I suggest, at times of danger, even more than in times of relative peace and safety, a scepticism, not a credulity, toward *form*—both political form, and also, because the two are inseparable, media form—if we are to safeguard, as we must, our ability to be critical of political content. It is worth remembering here Maurice Bloch's definition of ritual (closely associated with myth) as "the use of form for power" (1989: 45). Dare we relax our suspicion of "form" in an age of media spectacle (Kellner, 2003)? Dare we ignore, as mainstream media subsequently[4] appear to have done, the voices of those who seriously tried to challenge the exclusions of the G-8 Summit agenda, for example, the Dissent network? Dare we ignore the strategies of the spectacular UK state, which in a major denial of civil liberties, had the Dissent protesters physically confined by police in their improvised camp miles from the Gleneagles Summit?[5] I suggest not.

The Theoretical Stakes

What is at stake, theoretically, in moving toward media research that is decentered in the sense already explained? I suggested earlier that this move might facilitate dialogue with the wider social sciences about the mechanisms through which media messages get embedded in social life and about how, therefore, media contributes to the sustaining (or otherwise) of social order.

The problem of order is an old one in social theory, some would argue "the most fundamental for social theory" (Wrong, 1994: 1). It is a problem whose very formulation is entangled in metaphors so naturalized that we barely see them as metaphors: "The term 'structure' is so widely used in all disciplines to refer to any and all entities and phenomena that it has acquired an abstractness obscuring its metaphorical character" (Wrong, 1994: 4).

We have already seen, when discussing functionalism, the importance of freeing our thinking about the social world from hidden metaphors, but the problem goes wider. There are, as Wrong notes, a number of traps to avoid in thinking about social order. First, we must keep separate the motivation/value dimension of the question from the knowledge dimension. Some theorists emphasize the emotional drives toward social order, others the cognitive, and sociologists such as Durkheim emphasize both at various times (cf. Couldry, 2003a: 8–9). Media institutions are clearly involved in both cognitive and emotional dimensions of social belonging, and we should not analyze one contribution to the exclusion of the other. Second, we should avoid building our expected solutions into the way we formulate the problem: if we assume in advance that societies are held together by values, then we are likely to find them and quickly move on to assume it is those values that are key determinants of social cohesion, while possibly more important determinants are invisible to us because of how we posed the problem.[6] What's necessary, in other words, is to pose the question of social order in the most open way possible, which means social theorists being as open as possible about the nature of media's possible contribution and media theorists being as open as possible about the contribution of factors other than media.

Third, Wrong argues, we must avoid reducing in advance the scale on which we pose the problem of order. As Wrong puts it, "What are the relevant units [of explanation]?" (1994: 5). Order and disorder may occur on multiple scales; and we can envisage disorder on one level and order on another. A scale that has become particularly controversial recently is the national, that is, the very idea of national "societies as distinct, discrete entities forming coherent wholes or systems" (Wrong, 1994: 8). Once again, media are crucial in considering how scales beyond the national have become salient in questions of social order (Beck, 2000a; Urry, 2000) although, for many purposes, media cultures remain distinctly national.

Fourth, as Wrong puts it, there is the question of what constitutes disorder: Is it the war of all against all (Hobbes-style), or the "state of nature" (Rousseau), or a mixture of order and disorder rather like contemporary social life? We can put this another way: What degree of order should we expect in contemporary societies; and is there, as found in discussing the myth of the mediated center, a mismatch between *rhetorics* of order (claims made by particular institutions about their contributions to order) and reality? To confuse the two would be disastrous if, as Ernesto Laclau has argued, the growing complexity of contemporary societies *incites* more and more claims to or myths about order: "[Contemporary societies] are required by their very dynamics to become increasingly mythical" (Laclau, 1990: 67). Distinguishing myth (including media myths) from reality is, it follows, an issue of wide importance for social theory.

Given these difficulties even in formulating the question of social order, it is not surprising that different social theorists have taken very different views on *whether* social life is ordered and whether sociology's old reference point (the national society) any longer constitutes the nexus of relations and bonds that explains the happenings of daily life. Take, for example, recent French sociology. On the one hand, as is well known, Pierre Bourdieu's work (e.g., Bourdieu et al., 1999), in loyalty to the French sociological tradition from Durkheim, emphasizes the overwhelming importance of social structure in shaping the range of possibilities within which individuals can act. On the other hand, Alain Touraine's vision is not of social reproduction but of "desocialization" (2000: 5; cf. Bauman, 2001). Touraine sees culture as no longer a shared framework of values but "a set of resources and models which social actors seek to manage, to control and which they appropriate, whose transformation into social organisation they negotiate among themselves" (1988: 8; cf. Dubet, 1994: 30). The Tourainian tradition, instead of analyzing the role of *shared* categories of thought and action in social reproduction, insists on studying "that part of the subject [sociology] which is manifested in a *distance* from social categories" (Dubet, 1995: 103, added emphasis).

With the Bourdieu and Touraine traditions apparently locked in a deadly embrace of opposites, we might want to look elsewhere for a way forward. The work of the German social theorist Karin Knorr-Cetina (2001) is helpful. Far from a complete breakdown of social reproduction à la Bauman or Touraine, Knorr-Cetina sees new mechanisms of reproduction: "The retraction of social principles leaves no holes ... in the fabric of cultural patterns. There has been no loss of texture for society, though *what the texture consists of* may need rethinking" (2001: 527, added emphasis). Crucially for us here, Knorr-Cetina sees this transformed social space as marked by the new "pervasiveness of images themselves in a media and information society" (2001: 527), from which are built up what she vividly calls "unfolding structures of absences" (2001: 527–529), such as the rarely satisfied need to keep up to date with the latest computer software!

If our understanding of the fabric of social space is so uncertain, or at least contested, then the explanatory role of the individual becomes, potentially, crucial. At the very least, we need to know much more about the various things people do to *generate* order in their daily life. This includes their media consumption but, of course, many other factors, too. The call to think about how media consumption fits into the interlocking patterns of daily life goes back at least to Janice Radway (1988) and was echoed, as we saw, in British audience research (Silverstone 1994).

Here there are links to be made to interesting new research in France, as yet untranslated, on the *social* underpinnings of the individual (Martuccelli, 2002). What is useful about this work is its careful distinguishing between the factors, operating on a variety of scales, that sustain the individual: from psychological and material supports, to the more or less fluid roles available to actors, to social respect, to the particular strategies that individuals make to construct for themselves an identity as well as a protected space of *subjectivity*, that is, a space for action free from social direction or monitoring. Even more useful is that Martuccelli never romanticizes individual tactics or assumes the individual is free of social constraints; on the contrary, the individual must draw on resources that are social (transindividual) in nature, and the spaces of identity and subjectivity are defined by reference to their demarcation from social spaces. Less helpful, as already noted, is Martuccelli's lack of interest in media materials as possible components in the sustaining of individuals, which derives perhaps from his aim of de-emphasizing the pressures toward socialization he sees as hardwired into sociology's traditional explanatory model.

Ignoring media when thinking about individual strategies to create social order no doubt goes too far, just as did 1980's cultural studies when it overemphasized viewers' freedom to negotiate power through the dissident readings of media texts (I mean the often harsh and unfair debates provoked by John Fiske's notion of semiotic democracy; Fiske, 1987). Equally, it would be wrong to reduce the individual to a cipher reproducing social structure or media ideology. The best way forward lies, perhaps, in acknowledging more flexibility than we previously realized in how to think about media's possible contribution(s) to social order. If the social sciences can drop their secret Hegelianism, "which sees society as derived from the state's claim to embody the principle of order" (Beck, 2000a: 80), then media research should happily drop its own Hegelianism that installs the media (whether in general or in any particular manifestations) as the principal factor in explaining social change. A decentered media research can explore more openly how media *might* (as Knorr-Cetina puts it) be crucially involved in "filling in" the "texture" of the social world and shaping, both negatively and positively, the individual's space of action.

Let us now track this point more closely by considering what happens to the traditional agenda of media research.

A New Map of Media Studies

How might the landscape of media studies (both its recent past and its future research priorities) look if we decentered media research?

Such a move would compel us to find out much more about the relative importance in people's lives of (1) mainstream media institutions, (2) other media productions, and (3) nonmedia influences, and to understand better the range of variation here among individuals, groups, and classes. The range of media is, of course, increasing, so the complexity of their potential interactions increases exponentially (in that sense, the mediated environment in many parts of the world is supersaturated), with the result that the variety of paths individuals *might* choose across the media environment is huge, including paths along which media have minimal direct significance. The task is to understand how media density differs between my living space and yours, this work environment or leisure context and that one. Along these three axes—engagement, selection, spatial distribution—we need to know more about the variation between individuals' and groups' orientations to media.

The map of the resulting landscape of media research (present and future) has two crucial landmarks (*knowledge* and *agency*) that imply a third (*ethics*). Remember also that, from a decentered perspective, the map's border to the wider questions (just discussed) of media's role in social order is not closed.

Knowledge

By knowledge, I mean, not our knowledge of media as researchers, but the relationship between media and the distribution of social knowledge. The analysis of media forms in themselves, particularly relatively new forms such as reality television, remains important, of course; but from the perspective of a decentered media studies, it may be more important to analyze the role, if any (and there could be huge variation here), of media, both generally and specifically, in people's acquisition and use of knowledge, including knowledge of the social world.

This is an area where much important empirical work has been done in recent years: for example, the Glasgow Media Group's work on media influence on audience understanding of public issues (see Kitzinger, 1999, for a useful summary), on media and the economy (Gavin, 1999), and on media's relation to public opinion generally (Gripsrud, 1999; Lewis, 2001).

The work of the Glasgow Media Group has been particularly impressive in investigating systematically, across a range of issues, how patterns in news coverage are traceable in citizens' talk, interpretation, and (most originally) narratives of public events. The difficulties of tracing effects of media discourse do not disappear, of course, but the only way forward is to approach them from as many angles as possible. Here, though, my interest is less in methodological questions[7] and more in the general *direction* of this research. Public knowledge is surely an unavoidable question toward which media research should orient itself (cf. Corner, 1995); if we cannot say anything about media's possible contribution to the distribution of knowledge of the world in which we act, then something fundamental is missing (cf. Kitzinger, 1999: 17).

Yet it is clear there are a number of issues on which further research is needed: first, about the uses toward which media-sourced knowledge is put (or indeed not put) by individuals and groups across a range of real-life contexts; second, about the status of media relative to other potential sources of knowledge or authoritative information, both when information is originally acquired and when it is later put back into circulation (in argument, in self-presentation, and so on). Third, developing from the second, we need to know much more about the less explicit, more embedded, and naturalized use of mediated *knowledge* in everyday interaction and thought, again across a range of contexts (including those of media production, which is where the causal loop turns back onto itself). There is value here, as discussed in more detail in the next chapter, in rethinking Durkheim's notion of the social "category" to grasp the more systematic dimensions of the media's contribution to how the social world is constructed. Whether Durkheim or perhaps other models help us most can perhaps be left open; it is more important to recognize that, if media play a significant role in influencing the circulation of knowledge, then media studies has much to contribute to a renewed sociology of knowledge.

Agency

If one key focus of media research is knowledge (what do media contribute to the knowledge agents have of the world in which they act?), another is agency itself. Nicholas Garnham expressed this well in a critical discussion of audience research: "The point is not whether the audience is active or passive, but rather the fields of action which are opened up or closed down" (1999a: 118). Larry Grossberg had, from a different perspective, already made a similar point: "We need ... not a theory of audiences, but a theory of the organization and possibilities of agency at specific sites in everyday life" (1992: 341). Accumulating evidence about how people read or engage with this or that text is not, by itself, sufficient unless it contributes to our understanding of how they act in the social and personal world, with *or without* reference to media. I return to this point in chapter 5, in the context of the concern in cultural studies with political agency and the future of democratic politics.

Agency can, of course, be researched at many levels. Taking the obvious starting point for media-oriented research, we need more research on how (under what conditions and with what result) people exercise their agency in relation to *media flows*. There is the basic, but vital, question of how people select from what is potentially offered or (more drastically) how they screen out media that are imposed upon them (in public or working spaces, or within the constraints of their homes). There is the question also of how people allocate their attention and emotional investments among the media they happen to consume; there is a great difference between media that merely pass before us and media with which we sense a strong connection (whether public or private). Fan studies have done much to explore this difference,[8] but the difference arises in contexts other than fandom. Such questions become more difficult as the media environment itself becomes more complex and multilayered (spanning the full spectrum from the low-level interactivity of a flight-booking website to the intense concentration of a major sporting event, where television viewing may also be supplemented by online information streams, some of them interactive).

We need also to understand better how media contribute to people's agency across various institutional spheres outside media. Every sphere of life requires separate study; this is something we will explore in more detail in chapter 3. Here we can build on a literature that has grown in the 1990s on how people think or, in some cases, find it difficult to think about their own media consumption (Press, 1991; Seiter, 1999; Schroder, 2000; Hoover, Schofield Clark, and Alters, 2003). There is the difficult question here of how media might *diminish* people's sense of agency. The assumption has usually been that media are at worst neutral in this regard and at best add to people's possibilities for agency (e.g., Scannell, 1996). This, however, ignores another possibility, which is that the structured asymmetry of media communication works to limit at least some people's sense of agency, just as happens in the structured asymmetry of work and class relations (Couldry, 2000a: 22; cf. Sennett and Cobb, 1972; Murdock, 2000). Lembo's (2000) work on the problematic relations between media and agency is particularly interesting because he suggests that the social *appearance* of media contents may be misleading if we are looking for connections to social *agency*.

Related to agency is the more general question of how media connect to *belief*: people's belief about, or trust in, the authority of institutions (state, school, religious institutions). Indeed, once media research is genuinely decentered, people's beliefs about, or even orientation toward, *media* institutions need no longer be assumed, but can be problematized, making the whole field of media-oriented belief more interesting; what, for example, of those who have only a minimal orientation to media, or for whom media consumption is easily detached from the rest of their lives.

At this point, new types of questions come into view. If we have opened up for research the field of media-oriented belief (and so allowed for the possibility that the field is highly uneven, with many shades of belief and unbelief, engagement and disengagement, across families, groups, whole societies), then a comparative research agenda can be formulated. How far are different media territories, operating under specific historical trajectories and with different institutional balances between state, market, and civil society (Hallin and Mancini, 2004),[9] characterized by different average levels, and distributions, of what in short we might call *media belief.* How can we assume that the media culture—the intensity and density of beliefs about the legitimacy of media institutions, celebrity culture and the like—is the same in the United States, United Kingdom, Sweden, or Iran? Clearly, we cannot yet because the question of media belief has rarely even been broached as a topic.[10]

If we are opening out questions of media-oriented belief and agency on a global basis, then we also need to explore another dimension of comparison: people's degrees of agency in relation to the media process itself. In earlier work, I approached this from the point of view of people without any significant media resources who attempted to interrupt the media process for protest purposes (Couldry, 1999; 2000, part 3; 2001a). There is more broadly a growing international literature on alternative media (e.g., Downing, 2001; Rodriguez, 2001; Atton, 2001; and essays in Couldry and Curran, 2003), although this topic was for a long time marginalized in communications research. Here, however, it is important to close the causal loop and study what traces alternative media leave in the everyday practice of audiences (Downing, 2003), which takes us back to wider questions of social and political agency.

My choice of the word *agency* is, of course, not innocent any more than was my choice of *knowledge.* We need knowledge to have a chance of acting effectively as citizens of a democracy (or as people struggling to achieve a democracy); and agency, of course, is even more fundamental. Its importance derives from the principle that citizens should be free to contribute to decisions about, and ultimately change in, the conditions under which their lives are lived; *agency,* in other words, is the crucial term in clarifying why citizens should be knowledgeable and about what, and thereby underpins the value of democracy itself.

Ethics

Researching media from the perspective of knowledge and agency raises questions about the media's contribution to the conditions under which any of us can act. Acting involves reflecting on how we should act, reviewing the relations between our knowledge, words, and actions. Knowledge and agency, as themes, inevitably therefore lead to questions of ethics.

Discussion about media's ethical implications in media studies has normally been limited to the stance we should take on questions of media power. Much less debated and much more contentious are explicit questions of media ethics. These come more easily into view, once we abandon the assumption that today's centralized system of media production and distribution is the only possibility. For within a decentered media research we now can freely ask: what are the ethical implications of the media we *currently* have? Or, as I have put it elsewhere, "Can we imagine a social world in which mediation is characterized by a different, more even, distribution of symbolic power?" (Couldry, 2003a: 138). Aspects of such a debate have, of course, been under way for some time, for example, in relation to Habermas's concept of the public sphere; but that debate has largely been about media's contribution to political deliberation. This is not the only, or even the most, important dimension of media ethics.

Ethics is about the type of life it is good to lead, so an ethics of media, at its simplest, would concern the contribution of media production/consumption, under prevailing conditions, to the good life of each person. Difficult ethical questions arise about the extent to which in societies saturated by media a good life should be a public one, that is, to some degree mediated; difficult moral questions arise about the grounds on which it is right to impose media publicity on another without that person's full consent (cf. O'Neill, 1990). Even more difficult ethical and moral questions arise about the long-term consequences for our possibiliites of agency of how media tend to cover public matters, such as war or human disasters (Robins, 1995; Boltanski, 1999; Silverstone, 2003). What has been lacking so far, however, is any overarching ethical framework for debating these and similar issues.

The difficulty of those issues means they are best left until the end of the book. For now, let me make some introductory remarks that will serve as a link to that final chapter.

Derrida and Stiegler (2001: 60) are right to suggest that we are only at the very beginnings of articulating what "an instrumental culture of film and television" today would involve. By this they mean, I suspect, not just a technical literacy about how media are put together or even the ability to deconstruct critically the hidden assumptions of a news report, but also the ability to live within a media-saturated environment in a critical way that safeguards our ability to act effectively as ethical beings (cf. Stiegler, 2004). A decentered and suitably sceptical agenda of media research can contribute to that debate because it starts out from reflections (not assumptions) about media's social *centrality*. It is thereby able to register and research people's own scepticism toward media, their attempts to distance themselves from media, their media literacy in this broader sense. We can investigate how members of the audience, in the course of their daily lives, *manage* their relations with media flows: our emerging sense of the *everyday ethics* of media consumption (cf. Hoover, Schofield Clark, and Alters, 2003) can then feed into our framework for thinking about the ethics of media production/circulation at a more theoretical level, the topic to which we devote the book's final chapter.

Conclusion

This chapter began with the challenge of how to listen differently to the noise and din of a media-saturated environment. In what, for some, will seem a paradoxical move, it has explored what it means to decenter media research, as a way of opening up both wider and different questions about how media fits, or does not fit, into the rest of our lives. The negative, deconstructive part of the chapter considered the problems in two ways of thinking about media that a decentered media research would want to move beyond: mediacentrism and the myth of the mediated center.

The positive part of the chapter has explored what a map of decentered media research priorities would look like. This map has two main features. First, it is not sealed off from the wider terrain of social research but can contribute to questions about social order that are currently unresolved within social theory, and where media clearly have considerable relevance. Second, and moving across to the terrain more usually associated with media studies, a decentered approach emphasizes not media as such (media texts and how they are produced, media texts and how they are interpreted) but broader questions of knowledge and agency. From this vantage point, the ethical dimensions of everyday life come into view and the question of how media institutions do, or do not, contribute to the conditions of ethical action.

This may still seem like a strategy for abandoning all the achievements of media research to date and, in return, only obtaining promises of future discoveries. But that is a misreading. First, I am not saying that the existing traditions of textual, institutional, or audience analysis have no place in media research; of course, they do, and they have a vital place. I am saying only that they are no longer the point of origin from which the research agendas of media studies should be constructed; there are now more interesting places from which to start. Second, the type of media research suggested here isn't, of course, entirely new; it builds on a shift in direction already under way in media and communications studies for at least a decade. This is a shift toward thinking about media less as text or institution (that is, as a readily demarcated *site* of analysis) and more as a force field within a complex space of social practice, much of it *not* directly related to media at all. I explain this paradigm shift in more detail in the next chapter.

Notes

1. Or the economy, or social psychology, if we want media research to move toward those disciplines; but, insofar as media research in the United Kingdom has been oriented toward a social science discipline, it has generally been sociology, and that is my orientation, too.

2. For a classic version of this myth, see Shils (1975).

3. There are analogies here with recent deconstructions of the term *culture*: see Clifford (1990).

4. I say *subsequently* because before and in the immediate aftermath of the G-8 summit there was some scepticism in media news and comment about the substance of Blair's G-8 rhetoric, and particularly what difference it would make to lives in Africa; see, for example, Kamau and Burkeman (2005).

5. For details, see http://www.indymedia.org.uk/en/regions/scotland.

6. See Mann (1970) for a classic deconstruction along these lines of theories of the cohesion of 1960s British society.

7. For more discussion, see Couldry (forthcoming).

8. See Barker and Brooks (1998) and Harrington and Bielby (1995) for very open-minded empirical accounts.

9. We might also add religious institutions.

10. For details of a pioneering conference on media and belief organized by Waddick Doyle at the American University of Paris in March 2005, see http://www. aup.fr/news/pastconf/programs/2005_mediabelief.htm.

3
Theorizing Media as Practice

⟿

Should the past history of media research determine its current priorities? Not necessarily. This chapter attempts to formulate a new paradigm of media research that can draw together some of the more interesting recent work, but at the same time achieve a decisive break with some unprofitable disputes of the past. This new paradigm sees media not as text or production economy, but first and foremost *as practice*. Some of the stimulus for this comes from the recent growth of "practice theory" in sociology; indeed this new paradigm insists on a much closer relationship with central debates in the social sciences than previously in media studies, with the advantage that the major contribution of media research to those wider social science debates becomes clearer.

This is no place for a history of media research. To set the scene, however, it is worth recalling that theoretical discussion about the social consequences of media goes back well into the nineteenth century (Tocqueville 1994 [1835–40]; Kierkegaard 1962 [1846–47]), although it remained completely marginal in mainstream sociology until the mid-twentieth century with only rare exceptions (Tarde, 1969 [1922]). The contemporary landscape of media studies is the residue of at least five distinct currents of work: first, U.S. mass communications research, which was set firmly in the tradition of the experimental social sciences, but took its cue from wider intellectual debates on mass media and their consequences for democracy and social order; second, critical Marxist commentary, which also took its cue from mass culture debates, but within an agenda based on the critique of capitalism (this in turn developed into the political economy tradition); third, semiotic analysis, which in its dominant form developed in the context of European structuralism and poststructuralism and applied the most radical theoretical innovations of post–World War II literary theory to media texts; fourth, critical research, particularly on media audiences), which emerged in Britain in close association with semiotics and Marxism, but quickly developed into a broader empirical tradition that has continued through the 1990s; and fifth, and most recently, the line of anthropological research into media that has emerged out of postmodern versions of symbolic anthropology (Ginsburg, 1994; Ginsburg et al., 2002). Needless to say, there is not always common ground between these traditions: for example, the third has developed largely independently of the others with its own extensive theoretical framework drawing particularly on psychoanalysis, while the fourth is sharply critical of the first and second and has only a limited interest in the third; the fifth, meanwhile, has some difficulty acknowledging how much it has in common with the fourth (Abu-Lughod, 1999).

These traditions disagree, of course, as to their primary theoretical focus: for the first, it is problems of large-scale social effects; for the second, processes of commodification; for the third, the polysemy of the text; for the fourth, the process of interpretation; and for the fifth, open-ended practices of media production, circulation, and consumption. At the same time, there are, of course, cross currents: so the problems of the U.S. mass communications field with media effects have serious implications for critical theory and audience research, even if they are blissfully ignored by semiotic analysis while the process complexities uncovered by audience research are highly relevant for anthropological narratives of media practice. With such profusion, why call for a further paradigm? One aim is to put behind us some of the internecine disputes of the past (between audience research and Screen Theory over the determining status of the text: Morley, 1980; between audience research and political economy over the importance of audience practices of meaning-making (Garnham, 1995; Grossberg, 1995). Another aim is to help clarify where might lie the epicenter of new research questions, if (as I would argue) this no longer lies directly above the media text or the media's production economy.

The proposed new paradigm is disarmingly simple: it treats media as the open set of practices relating to, or oriented toward, media.[1] The potential of this reformulation becomes clear only when we look more closely at recent debates over practice in the social sciences. Its aim, however, is straightforward: to decenter media research from the study of media texts or production structures (important though these are) and to redirect it to the study of the open-ended range of practices focused directly or indirectly on media. This places media studies firmly within a broader sociology of action and knowledge (or cultural and cognitive anthropology) and sets it firmly apart from versions of media studies formulated within the paradigm of literary criticism.

Why Practice?

This proposal needs some unpacking, first, in terms of questions of media analysis and, second, in terms of questions of social theory.

Practice as an Emerging Theme in Media Research

The new paradigm decenters the media text for a reason: to sidestep the insoluble problems over how to prove media effects (i.e., a convincing causal chain from the circulation of a media text, or a pattern of media consumption, to changes in the behavior of audiences). The classic version of this debate concerned cultivation analysis: cultivation analysis has been unfairly vilified for at least being explicit and methodical in its attempt to prove a causal chain between heavy television viewing and cognitive and moral shifts in those viewers, which was extremely difficult to establish at a statistically significant level (Signorielli and Morgan, 1990). But hidden assumptions about media effects abound in media analysis and everyday talk about media. Indeed, they are hard to avoid if we start from the text itself: outside literary approaches, why *else* study the detailed structure of a media text as the primary research focus unless we can plausibly claim that those details make a difference to wider social processes? But it is exactly this that is difficult to show. As Justin Lewis put it: "The question that should be put to textual analysis that purports to tell us how a cultural product 'works' in contemporary culture is almost embarrassingly simple: where's the evidence? Without evidence, everything else is pure speculation" (Lewis, 1991: 49). Ultimately, the question of media effects cannot be avoided,[2] but its difficulty encouraged many researchers to shift their priorities elsewhere.

A popular alternative has been to start from the institutional structures that produce media, as in the political economy and (more recently) the cultural economy traditions (Garnham, 1990; Du Gay, 1997; Hermann and McChesney, 1997; Hesmondhalgh, 2002; Curran and Seaton, 2003). Clearly, the analysis of industrial and market structures in the media and cultural sectors is valid in its own right, as a contribution to policy debates and to the analysis of the wider economy, as well as being vital to our understanding of the pressures that limit participation in those sectors on various scales and also limit the range of outputs they produce. Here, there is no question of speculation (quite the contrary) and on any view such work is important. But in considering what should be the *general* paradigm for media research and media theory, there is a difficulty in situating it exclusively in media production. The structures of media production, and particularly the dynamics of concentration and conglomeration, do not, of themselves, tell us anything about the uses to which media products are put in social life generally. Even from a Marxist perspective, which insists on the causal primacy of economic relations, it is difficult to make the leap from arguing that (1) economic factors determine the nature of media production, to arguing that (2) the (economically determined) nature of media production determines the *social* consequences of media texts. Unlike when we are analyzing general labor conditions, there is a crucial uncertainty about *how* media texts (or any texts produced in an economy) causally mediate between the world they represent and the world where they are consumed. This was precisely the force of the challenge (noted in the last chapter) to the dominant ideology thesis (Abercrombie et al., 1981): where is the evidence that the holding of beliefs associated with a dominant ideology adds anything to the structuring of social relations by the dull compulsion of economic life (Marx)? The point applies a fortiori if we consider the consequences of media texts, since the relationship between consumption of a media text (however it may be *read* as reproducing an ideology) and transmission of belief in that ideology is also uncertain (cf. the Justin Lewis quote in the previous paragraph). Unless therefore we reduce media texts to being a conduit for economic signals (absurd in all but the crudest case), we are forced once again, even within a political economy model, to consider what people "do with" media.

This, after all, was the point of audience research—to emphasize that consumption is a "determinate moment" in the production of meaning through media texts (Hall, 1980). The only problem was that audience research developed in an intellectual landscape in Britain decisively influenced by semiotics, requiring that all questions about media start from the supposed structuring properties of the text itself. David Morley's and Roger Silverstone's work was decisive in broadening this emphasis (Morley, 1986, 1992; Silverstone, 1994), but as time went on, the connection of audience research (from fan practices to video use) to the moment of textual consumption was increasingly loosened until the audience become undecidable—undecidable, that is, in relation to the original moment of textual consumption (Ang, 1996: 70). The problem was that audience research remained constrained by its primary emphasis on people's relationships to texts.

It is to escape that constraint that my proposed paradigm starts not with media texts or media institutions, but with practice—not necessarily the practice of *audiences* (I'll come back to this), but media-oriented practice, in all its looseness and openness. What, quite simply, are people *doing* in relation to media across a whole range of situations and contexts?

Like any new paradigm that seeks to resolve a crisis or contradiction in how a field of research is constructed, this paradigm was "at least partially anticipated" (Kuhn, 1970: 75), in this case in the 1990s. First, there was important research into the whole range of domestic practices in which television viewing was inserted (Silverstone, 1994; Silverstone and Hirsch, 1992). This work developed a rich theoretical framework drawing on recent developments in sociology of science and technology and encompassing the latest developments in the sociology of the family and social anthropology. The focus remained the home, as the primary site of media consumption, although there was a less noticed line of research on public viewing of television (Lemish, 1982; Krotz and Tyler Eastman, 1999; McCarthy, 2002).

The new paradigm was anticipated, secondly, by researchers who sought to move beyond the specific contexts of media consumption. Having concluded that "television's meanings for audiences ... cannot be decided upon outside of the multidimensional intersubjective networks in which the object is inserted and made to mean in concrete contextual settings" (Ang, 1996: 70), Ien Ang posed the different question of "what it means, or what it is like, to live in a media-saturated world" (1996: 72). My own early research inflected this general question from the perspective of power, asking "what it means to live in a society dominated by large-scale media institutions" (Couldry, 2000a: 6). The shift to a more widely focused research question was anticipated also by the emergence of the term *mediation* (Silverstone, forthcoming; Meyrowitz, 1994) to refer to the broad expanse of social processes focused around media, even if the first prominent use of that term (Martin-Barbero, 1993) was concerned, still, with extending our understanding of media *consumption* to encompass a broader range of cultural participation. It is here that recent anthropological research into media processes, free as it is from any primary attachment to studying texts and their interpretation, has become a promising ally, while at the same time acquiring a higher profile in anthropology itself.

Important also were two explicit attempts to shift the paradigm of media research in the late 1990s. Coming from outside media studies, Abercrombie and Longhurst (1998) challenged what they saw as a paradigm of media research dominated by ideological questions (the "incorporation/resistance" paradigm) and proposed to replace it by a "spectacle/performance" paradigm that foregrounded the *various* levels of engagement people have to different aspects of media culture. While this proposal was valuable for drawing on a wider frame of historical, cultural, and sociological reference than usual in media research, a problem was its downgrading of questions of power, which itself made some contestable assumptions about how power works in media-saturated spaces. Around the same time came the proposal that we were now entering the "third generation" of audience research

(Alasuutaari, 1999) whose priority was to "get a grasp on our contemporary 'media culture'" (1999: 6), for example, through an interest in the open-ended processes of identity construction linked to media (Hermes, 1999); but this "generational" formulation risked disguising the radical nature of the shift under way by holding onto the notion of audiences as its central focus.

Perhaps, however, the definitive formulation of the emerging paradigm shift under way came with the media anthropologist Liz Bird's recent book (Bird, 2003), the first chapter of which announces a new approach "beyond the audience" that aims to address "the amorphous nature of media experience," arguing that "we cannot really isolate the role of media in culture, because the media are firmly anchored into the web of culture, although articulated by individuals in different ways…. The 'audience' is everywhere and nowhere" (Bird, 2003: 2–3).

It is worth noting, however, that Bird makes a crucial qualification: "Our culture may be 'media saturated,' but as *individuals* we are not, or at least not in any predictable, uniform way" (2003: 3, added emphasis). There is the beginning of a separation here between our concern with a media-saturated culture and our interest in the specificity of local experience. The term *culture* has its own problems if it implies a holistic notion of a distinct cultural system (Hannerz, 1992). This suggests that, in formulating a new paradigm of media research, we should take in the whole range of practices in which media consumption and media-related talk are embedded, including practices of avoiding, or selecting out, media inputs (Hoover, Schofield Clark, and Alters, 2003); such practices may not be part of what normally we refer to as "media culture," but as practices *oriented* to media they are hardly trivial. This, it might seem, loosens the tie to media texts too much and plunges us into chaos. Fortunately, however, the recent emergence of a *practice*-based research paradigm in sociology ensures that we need not be left floating without theoretical moorings.

The Sociology of Practice

The recent shift toward practice in some social sciences has long philosophical roots (e.g., Wittgenstein, Merleau-Ponty, Nietzsche) and is the latest in a series of attempts to overcome the old theoretical division between structure and agency (Bourdieu, 1977); for authoritative overviews of the term *practice* overall, see Schatzki (1999) and Reckwitz (2002). There is no space to go into this background here. The key question, instead, is what the notion of practice offers to media sociology. There are three important points to be made.

First, as the American sociologist Ann Swidler (2001) explains, the aim of practice theory is to replace an older notion of "culture"—as internal "ideas" or "meanings" of a defined group—with a different analysis of culture in terms of two types of publicly observable processes: first, *practices* themselves, particularly "routine activities (rather than consciously chosen actions) notable for their unconscious, automatic, un-thought character" (2001: 74); and, second, *discourse*, which "is not [just] what anyone says, but the system of meanings that allows them to say anything at all" (2001: 75). While we might query Swidler's exclusive emphasis on routine activities (what about discourses of reflexivity?), and while we might also query the term *system* in the characterization of discourse (it would be better, perhaps, to refer to *principles of ordering*, without assuming that order or system is necessarily achieved in discourse; see chapter 2), nonetheless, this represents a useful, pragmatic shift in the analysis of culture, including media culture. If recent media research has foregrounded media culture, practice theory translates this into two concrete and related questions: What types of things do people do in relation to media? And what types of things do people say in relation to media?[3]

Second, practice research aims to be as open as possible in analyzing what practices are out there, which in turn depends on how people *understand* what actions constitute a distinct practice—a complex question because actions are linked to a practice not just by explicit understandings but also through being governed by common rules and sharing the common reference point of certain ends, projects, and beliefs (Schatzki, 1999: 89). There undoubtedly *are* a whole mass of media-oriented practices in contemporary societies, but how they are divided into specific practices and how those practices are coordinated remain an open question.

We cannot resolve such questions here. What matters is taking this question as our starting point, since it distances us from the normal media studies assumption that what audiences do ("audiencing") *is* a distinctive set of practices rather than an artificially chosen "slice" through daily life that *cuts across* how they actually understand the practices in which they are engaged (cf. Grossberg's and Radway's classic critiques: Grossberg [1987]; Radway [1988]). If we live in a media-saturated world, then it is reasonable to expect that *how* such a world is carved up into recognizable practices may no longer correspond to categorizations formed in a "presaturation" world (when audiencing could be assumed to be a discrete activity). But—and this is the point that practice theory makes clear—to establish what *are* the new principles by which practices oriented to media are demarcated, we cannot read them from the surface descriptions attached by media discourse. We must look closely at the categorizations of practice that people make themselves.

Third, the space of practices is not as chaotic as might appear, for the crucial reason that practices are organized among themselves. How this works is the fundamental question that Swidler addresses: "How [do] some practices anchor, control, or organise others?" (2001: 79). Put in these stark terms, this is a surprisingly difficult question. Swidler approaches it, first, from the point of view of definitional hierarchy (some practices are defined as part of a larger practice that provides their key reference points; so, for example, political marketing, lobbying, and campaigning are part of the wider practice of politics); but second, as a question of dynamic change (some practices "anchor" others because changes in the former automatically cause a reformulation of the latter's aims). For the second case, Swidler makes an interesting suggestion that "public ritual" has a crucial role to play in "the visible, public enactment of new patterns so that 'everyone can see' that everyone else has seen that things have been changed" (2001: 87). Some practices, in other words (although this is my gloss, not Swidler's), work to *enact* new forms of categorization and distinction replied upon in other practices.

One of Swidler's examples is how the public performance of identity based on sexuality in the San Francisco's Lesbian/Gay Pride Parade (from 1971 onward) changed the conditions in which sexual identity in San Francisco could be claimed and expressed more generally. Swidler argues that anchoring practices are associated particularly with the management of conflict and difference but that, once established, the principles enacted by those practices become part of the social "structure" itself.

As Swidler herself makes clear, these suggestions are tentative, and much more work in this area is needed, but this practice-based approach is suggestive of how we might understand the relation of media-oriented practices to social practice as a whole. What if one of the main things media do is anchor other practices through the "authoritative" representations and enactments of key terms and categories that they provide? Some questions, then, if we theorize media as practice, are how, where, and for whom this anchoring role works and with what consequences for the organization of social action as a whole?

Media as Practice

Having now set the scene, I want to explore (inevitably schematically) what a theory of media as practice might be like, and what its key questions might be. As we have seen, this paradigm is not fundamentally new, but it is distinctive in being formulated without any reliance on textual or political economy models and with enough generality to be open to wider developments in sociology and anthropology. As John Tulloch (2000: 19–32) has argued, media research and theory need to be more closely integrated with the wider social sciences (although this requires some rapprochement on their part as well!)—this is much more productive, I would add, than relying on the abstractions of philosophy or philosophically generated theories about media (whether Heidegger's philosophy of Being, Baudrillard's polemics, or Deleuze and Guattari's conceptual explorations). Media theory has no independent value as theory; it is valuable only when it helps us formulate better questions for empirical research.

To flesh out how a theory of media as practice shifts the priorities of media research, I want to discuss three consequences of this emphasis: antifunctionalism, openness to the variable and complex organization of practice, and an interest in the mechanisms through which practices are ordered. At this general level, media theory is no different from any other area of social theory, although media's role in *representing* the social world from which media are generated adds to the complexity of how their consequences can be understood. Media represent other practices and so have direct consequences for how those practices are defined and ordered.

Beyond Functionalism

I do not want to dwell long on this point, since we have discussed it in the last chapter. Indeed, functionalism is so long dead in sociology and anthropology that it is embarrassing to find it alive and well in areas of media research. Functionalism, as we saw, is the idea that large regions of human activity (societies, cultures, and so on) can best be understood as if they were self-sufficient, complex, functioning systems. Depending on taste, the metaphor of functioning can be biological (the natural organism, such as the human body) or technological (artificial systems, such as the machine). Societies, or cultures, are conceived in functionalist accounts as complex wholes formed of a series of parts, each of which functions by contributing to the successful working of the whole. Action at the level of society's or culture's parts has no unanticipated effects, or if it does, it is quickly absorbed back into the whole's wider functioning through positive feedback loops.

The main problem, however, lies with functionalism's underlying claim that there *are* such totalities as societies and cultures that function as working systems. The problem becomes clearer when this claim is applied in detail. We need go no further than Steven Lukes's (1975) classic deconstruction of functionalist accounts of political ritual, which analyze political rituals in terms of how they contribute to society's political "stability" by affirming certain central beliefs and values. But even if there are such centrally held beliefs and values, which Lukes also questions, this account begs deeper questions about "whether, to what extent, and in what ways society *does* hold together" (Lukes, 1975: 297). *Is there*, Lukes asks, a functioning social "whole" of which political rituals could be a "part"?

Yet functionalist explanations continue to crop up in media research in some surprising places.[4] The standard positions in debates about stardom and celebrity culture assume, at root, that the industrial production of celebrity discourse *must* contribute to some wider social "function," whether we call it identity formation or social integration or both. Here, for example, is McKenzie Wark: "We may not like the same celebrities, we may not like any of them at all, but it is the existence of a population of celebrities, about whom to disagree, that *makes it possible* to constitute a sense of belonging" (Wark, 1999: 33, my emphasis, quoted Turner et al., 2000: 14). Where is the evidence that people identify with celebrities in any simple way, or even that they regard celebrity culture as important, rather than a temporary distraction, let alone that celebrities make possible everyone's sense of belonging? The lack of *empirical* work here illustrates how functionalism closes down research options.

An advantage of starting with the practice question—what types of things do people do/say/think that are oriented to media?—is that there is no intrinsic plausibility in the idea that what people do (across a range of practices and locations) should add up to a functioning whole. Why should it? In the past, an apparent reason was that, without the ordering presence of "society" as a functioning whole, the meanings and mutual relationships of practices could not themselves be understood, agency being incomprehensible without structure. Giddens's structuration theory (1984), whatever detailed problems it raises, was a convincing move beyond that problem since it showed how principles of order could both produce, and be reproduced, at the level of practice itself (social order, in other words, is "recursively" present in practice and in the organization of practice: cf. Swidler, 2001: 78). Practice theory, indeed, seeks to develop this insight by insisting that "there is no reason to think that social life can exhibit [ordered] features only if it is a totality" (Schatzki, 1999: 10) and by exploring other ways of thinking about social order. Freed of functionalism, media research is able to offer new insight to such debates.

The Varieties of Media Practice

The value of practice theory, as we have seen, is to ask open questions about what people are doing and how they categorize what they are doing, avoiding the disciplinary or other preconceptions that would automatically read their actions as, say, "consumption" or "being-an-audience," whether or not that is how the actors see their actions. One possibility we need to be ready for—anticipated in the quotation from Ien Ang already given (1996: 70)—is that, in many cases, media consumption or audiencing can be understood only as part of a practice that is not itself "about" media: what practice this is depends on who we are describing and the context of description.

Watching a football game on television might for one person be best analyzed as part of an intensely emotional practice as a football fan, perhaps a fan of a particular team; for another, perhaps that person's partner or child, it may be an obligation or pleasure of their relationship together to share the first person's passion; for someone watching in a public space, it may be part of a practice of group solidarity; for a fourth, it may be something done to fill in time, instantly "put-downable" (cf. Hermes, 1995) as soon as a friend rings the doorbell or the person gets the energy to go back to some work. Pointing this out is hardly new, of course (Bausinger, 1984). What it demonstrates, however, is that the main priorities for media research cannot be the varieties of how people read the text of this televised game (since watching football on television is not the *practice* we are interested in analyzing) nor the structure of the televised game's text considered in itself.

It is more interesting to consider, first, the range of practices in which the act of watching this football game occurs and, second, the consequences of that common feature for the relationships between those practices. As to the first question, it will be only in the case of the football fan that the way he or she reads the game's text is likely to be of research interest since it is only here that the watching of the game forms a central, nonsubstitutable part of a wider practice. Political economy approaches are important background in all these cases, but again probably only vital background in the case of the football fan, since economic pressures have had a major effect on the places where televised games can be watched and even the structure of the game itself. As to the second question, the fact that people in performing a huge range of practices (from fandom to family interaction to group solidarity at a community center or pub to just waiting for something else to do) should *all* be doing the same thing at the same time is, however, significant for our understanding of the space/time coordination of practices through media. Similar questions could be asked of watching a prime-time news bulletin. Here there might be more commonality around the practice of watching the news (an inherently general activity that is, perhaps, a distinct practice for many people) than if we took reading a celebrity magazine, which is much more ambiguous (is it just passing time, a deliberate search for humor, or information seeking?). The answer can be given for particular individuals and groups only in the contexts of their everyday practice, which must take into account the contexts, if any, where knowledge of the contents of that celebrity magazine can later be put to use.

Clearly, this only begins to track the variety of media-oriented practices and media-oriented actions that form part of other practices. Large areas of this terrain have, of course, already been explored in media research, but there remain many areas that are still little known. To name a few:

- practices of using media sources in education;
- individuals' uses of media references in telling stories about themselves, their families, or historical events;
- the uses of media in the legal system and, indeed, in work practices across the public world (so far, most research has focused on the consequences of media for political practice, but there are many other areas worth investigating).

There is also the larger question of how media products and references to media are, over time, affecting practice in all fields of social life, which I have begun to explore elsewhere, drawing on Bourdieu's field theory (Couldry, 2003b). How have media, for example, reshaped the field of the visual arts; or moving well beyond the usual territory of cultural research, how have media reference points and, more specifically, the pressure to respond to news agendas, changed everyday practices in schools, hospitals, and law enforcement?

Focusing on practice is a more radical adjustment to our research agendas than might at first appear. It is commonplace to study talk shows, for example, as texts, but much less common to study them as a social practice whereby particular groups of people are brought together to perform before each other in a studio (but see for examples of a practice-based approach, Gamson, 1998; Grindstaff, 2002). The resulting media text (say, an episode of the *Jerry Springer Show*) is only one facet of the overall practice.

At this descriptive level, media consumption at least (media production is different, since it is generally a rationalized work practice) may seem frustratingly heterogeneous, rather than an ordered field. Its principles of order often derive, at least initially, from the order to be found in the various practices in which media consumption (and its uses) are inserted. But, as already suggested, media consumption (and production) may quite independently be important to understanding the common patterns between other practices. It is to questions of patterning and ordering that I wish to turn next.

The Ordering of Media Practice/Media's Ordering of Other Practices

We return here to the difficult question posed by the cultural sociologist Ann Swidler: how do some practices anchor other practices, producing a hierarchy of practices and also contributing to the structure within which those other practices occur and take their meaning? The case of media-oriented practices, however, raises a specific question: do media practices have a *privileged* role in anchoring other types of practice because of the privileged circulation of media representations and images of the social world? This is quite apart from questions about the internal hierarchies among media practices that, at least in forms such as the privileging of "live" media coverage over other types of media coverage, are relatively familiar. I am interested here in the more difficult question of the potential hierarchies between media practices and *other* sorts of practice. How can we investigate such a relationship, and what concepts do we need to clarify it?

Here we need to draw on another area of (this time, classical) social theory: Durkheim's concept of *social categories* (Durkheim, 1953). A social category for Durkheim is a concept that is involved in articulating (directly or indirectly) a society's order: such a category is put to work in formulating certain core understandings of how the social world works and the values on which it is based. A fundamental difference between Durkheim's theoretical framework and practice theory is that Durkheim assumes "society" as the fundamental entity underlying any sociological explanation, whereas practice theory does not. However, we can draw on Durkheim's insights without subscribing to his functionalist assumptions, in order to understand the categorical force of certain terms as they are mobilized in the *rhetorics* that media use to represent social reality and their privileged role as communicators of it. A nonfunctionalist approach may be able to explain the binding authority of certain media practices in relation to other practices via the notion of *ritual* (which, as we saw, Swidler herself introduces to explain how some practices anchor others, but without explaining the term). In ritual practices, wider patterns of meaning are recognized as being enacted, although not necessarily intended or articulated, by the performers (Rappaport, 1999: 24). Indeed, ritual is one important way in which the legitimacy of assumed wider values can be confirmed or communicated. Ritual practices are able to "frame" those wider values and thereby reproduce them as follows:

- the actions comprising rituals are structured around certain categories (often expressed through boundaries);
- those categories suggest, or stand in for, an underlying value;
- this value captures our sense that "the social" is "at stake" in the ritual.

As a result (recalling Swidler's language), ritual practices may anchor all sorts of other practices that deal in the same categories and values.

On what does the particular power of media-oriented rituals depend? There is no space to explain this in detail here,[5] but it is based on the fundamental categorical distinction between what is in the media and what is not in the media, which enables media representations to be seen as standing in for, or speaking authoritatively about, the nonmedia practices they represent. The "as seen on TV" label still seen on some supermarket goods is just the simplest version of this distinction in use, but it illustrates the anchoring role of media practices at work. The pervasiveness of celebrity culture (discourse about celebrity inside and outside media) is another example of such anchoring: even if, as already noted, it is uncertain how important celebrity discourse is in individuals' articulations of their identities, the *idea* that celebrity actions demand special attention is continuously reproduced. In that sense, celebrity actions can be said to anchor other practices by comprising a constant point of reference within them. These are just two examples of how the ritualized dimensions of media practice may have an ordering role in relation to other practices. The difficult question is how far this anchoring role extends across social practice in general; simply to identify such a role is not at all the same as saying celebrity discourse, let alone celebrities themselves, have a social function.

Clearly, we are here just at the edge of a large area of research. For now, the main point is that these research questions only emerge once we redefine the aim of media research as the analysis of media's consequences *for social practice as a whole,* studying the full range of practices oriented toward media (not just direct media consumption). It is important, however, to emphasize that, in researching the role of media practices and the products of media practices (images, representations, patterns of discourse) in ordering other practices across the social world, we are *not* giving up on the important concerns of historical media research with questions of representation, for the study of how particular media texts embody claims about the social world in regular ways will remain important for our understanding of media's consequences for social practice. Similarly, with the question of media effects and media power: reorienting the media research paradigm as I am proposing does not mean abandoning such larger questions but, on the contrary, attempting to answer them in more precise ways that are based in the details of everyday practice and its organization. The aim then is not to abandon the interests of previous media research, but to displace and broaden its focus from questions based on the consideration of texts (and how texts are interpreted or produced) to questions based on media practices' role in the ordering of social life more generally.

This, of course, is to put considerable weight on the term *ordering* (or in Swidler's language *anchoring*). I have already glossed this one way in terms of categories and rituals that are structured through categories. There are other ways, too, in which we might understand how certain practices order or anchor others. First, we might look at the coordinated networks between agents and things that Actor Network Theory analyzed. Let's think of the practices that together make up the "media profile" received by a major business corporation. They have an anchoring role in relation to the business strategies of that corporation, because of the "network" that links the actions of its executives, press office, key media contacts, major investors, and so on, when an announcement of a new strategy is made and the executives wait to see what media coverage it receives. Bad media coverage, because it is read by investors as negatively affecting the corporation's value as an investment, will constrain the corporation's future actions. Such actor networks involving media practices with an anchoring role have been little studied, but they are an important part of how many fields of practice are ordered. This is just one example of how the detailed study of practice (including actor networks) might illuminate our understanding of media's role in the ordering of social life more generally. Other conceptual links might be made here, for example, to Bourdieu's concept of habitus, which seeks to explain the underlying determinants of the practices that are available to different agents (Bourdieu, 1977; McNay, 1999). There are no doubt still other concepts that might be useful for specifying how anchoring might work that draw on alternative theoretical perspectives, for instance, Foucauldian perspectives, but there is no space to pursue these here.

The point, rather, is that we need the perspective of practice to help us address how media are embedded in the interlocking fabric of social and cultural life. This question, as I have suggested, cuts deeper than our sense of what it *feels* like to live in a media-saturated world, since it covers both cognitive and emotional dimensions to how practices are ordered; and in turn, through the link with cognitive questions (ways of thinking and categorizing the world), it links to the question of how practices oriented to media are differentially ordered for those with ready access to media resources (whether as media producers or as privileged media sources) and for those without. In this way, we can perhaps hope to develop a different approach toward understanding media's consequences for the distribution of social power.

Conclusion

I have tried to open out a direction for media theory, rather than map anything definitively. I have been interested throughout in theory not for its own sake but because it clarifies what questions are interesting for media research and how we might formulate that choice. Much of my argument has involved contextualizing a new research paradigm that theorizes media as practice, rather than as text or production process: what range of practices is oriented to media and what is the role of media-oriented practices in ordering other practices? This is, I believe, a more open and inclusive paradigm for media research than previous ones.

That paradigm draws for its theoretical tools much more on general social science than on media research—unsurprisingly, since it addresses questions no longer about media as such, or even about the direct consumption of media, but rather questions about the contributions media make to social practice more generally.

No new paradigm, as mentioned earlier, can be wholly new. Indeed, we return here to the spirit of Lazarsfeld and Merton's (1969 [1950]) exploratory remarks about mass media, made entirely within a social science perspective. Ironically, perhaps, this takes us back to the origins, if not the later versions, of U.S. communications research, the first stage of the historical sketch I offered at the start of this chapter. But if this is a return, it is a return reinforced by Latin American and European thinking about mediation and by a scepticism toward the classification of practice marked by late twentieth-century philosophy (whether we take Wittgenstein's *Philosophical Investigations* or Foucault's *The Order of Things* as our reference point). And, surprisingly, we return here to the question of media effects as well. For Lazarsfeld and Merton, the first, if most difficult, question of media effects was: what are "the effects of the existence of media in our society" (1969: 495, added emphasis)? Practice is perhaps the only concept broad enough to help us prise this question open.

Notes

1. A few years ago, I expressed this in terms of the study of 'the culture of media belief," but this now seems to me too limited in its selection from the wide field of media-oriented practices (Couldry 2000a).

2. I discuss possible approaches in Couldry (forthcoming).

3. Implied here also is studying what people believe and think, as evidenced by what they say and do (cf. chapter 2).

4. There may, indeed, be a deeper reason for this: compare Briankle Chang's argument that at the root of communication theory is "a certain hermeneutic ideology" that is "functionalist" because it "postulat[es] understanding as the norm, … and categoriz[es] any failure of understanding as incidental and anomalous' (Chang 1996: 174–175).

5. See Couldry (2003a).

PART II
Culture, Agency, Democracy

4
The Promise of Cultural Studies

᠎

I use the term "civility" to designate the speculative idea of a "politics of politics," or a politics in the second degree, which aims at creating, re-creating and conserving the set of conditions in which politics as a collective participation in public affairs is possible, or at least is not made absolutely impossible.

—Balibar, 2004: 115

Wherever we have started from, we need to listen to others who started from a different position.

—Williams 1958: 320

So far this book might appear to have focused on purely academic questions: What should be the priorities for media research? What theoretical framework is most appropriate for understanding media's social consequences? Implicitly, we have been concerned with questions of power insofar as they run throughout any analysis of media and culture, but we have not addressed politics directly, or even (in Balibar's phrase) the "politics of politics."

Of course, we could have made politics our explicit priority in discussing media, but then why go to such lengths to develop a *decentered* strategy of media research? Why not just ask straight off: What are the key features of mediated political rhetoric? What are the key features of how media institutions are currently representing politicians? Is corporate influence over media production growing? And so on. By contrast, the more indirect, decentered route toward understanding media offered here does not yield such immediate dividends. Its benefits can at best be long-term: an appreciation of the conditions under which media contribute to people's sense of themselves as effective and knowledgeable agents; a scepticism toward certain narratives of national "unity" in media, and so on.

In the next two chapters, we see how the themes of a decentered media research resonate in a context that is more explicitly political, the space of cultural studies. The shift from questions of media-specific research to cultural studies is a subtle, but important one. In the past,[1] I've argued for the status of cultural studies as a discipline (in order to foreground much needed methodological debate); to this extent, I have argued for cultural studies' roots as being in the sociology of culture and media. But here I am less interested in questions of disciplinary allegiance than in the dimension that *distinguishes* cultural studies from cultural sociology: its explicit value commitment to the in-depth study of culture's implications in power. From this perspective—I will try and unpack the values of cultural studies more explicitly later—a parallel between the research priorities already argued for and cultural studies' distinctive brand of reflexivity starts to emerge. In chapters 2 and 3, I emphasized the following questions:

1. On the theoretical level, how do media contribute to how social order is constructed, approaching this with a degree of scepticism toward powerful narratives of centralized order and a respect for complexity and multiplicity?
2. On the empirical level, do media contribute to people's knowledge and sense of agency, and what are the resulting implications of media for ethics?

Implicit already in these questions is one notion essential to the idea of a participative democracy: an interest in effective, knowledgeable agents across the whole of social space, not just in accredited "centers" of power. People require knowledge and a sense of agency if they are to be actively involved in determining what happens to them. An implicit value, then, of the decentered approach to media is to research what contribution media are actually *making* toward fulfilling the preconditions for the effective participative democracy valued by cultural studies.[2]

The link between media research and cultural studies extends further into questions of methodology. If I am suspicious about accounts of media that exaggerate their centrality and "functional" necessity, or exaggerate the prevalence of "order" in the social world, this is not just for reasons of theoretical precision. It is motivated also by an ethical concern: a concern to *hear* the range of voices that characterize the social terrain, and not reduce their complexity. But this concern overlaps with cultural studies' "politics":

its aim of responsibly accounting for others in its account of the social world (Couldry, 2000b: 126–130). We need to find a language of social description that is adequate to this complexity: on one side, a suspicion of reductive or simplifying accounts (what we might, adapting Christopher Norris (1987: chapter 8) a little mischievously,[3] call an "ethics of deconstruction"); on the other side, but inseparable from the first, a commitment to empirical rigor in building the accounts we do make of the social world (that draws on what we might, analogously, call an "ethics of construction"). These methodological issues may seem to be the exclusive concern of academics with the leisure to debate them, but they are not. For the complexity we miss when descriptively we "reduce" the social terrain is not a logical complexity, but a human complexity, a complexity of *voice*. Hearing that complexity requires a commitment to listen.[4] Voice, of course, is a value of effective democracy, too. So, in valuing voice, political and methodological concerns overlap.

Cultural studies, in this sense, is not a political flourish (whose disappearance would be as incidental to media and cultural research as its emergence). Cultural studies is the explicit conscience of responsible media and cultural research. It cannot, as I suspect some now hope, be abandoned in a side room like an unwelcome guest—without damaging the ethical basis of our whole research field.

Debate on this point is often obscured by disputes about this or that particular tributary of cultural studies and its methodological standards or political relevance. More productive, I suggest, is to focus on what, in good times and bad, is at stake in the *idea* of cultural studies, since it is here that cultural studies' promise continues to lie. If we return to the words of the first person explicitly to articulate that promise, Raymond Williams (cf. O'Connor, 2005), it will be easier to grasp how cultural studies can help address two linked challenges of the early twenty-first century: the crisis in the preconditions of democratic politics, and the lack of dialogue and mutual understanding that, in part (of course, it is only one of many factors), fuels the current global conflict.

The Values of Cultural Studies

What is cultural studies? I stand by the definition at the start of my previous book *Inside Culture: cultural studies* is a "space for sustained, rigorous, self-reflexive empirical research into the massive, power-laden complexity of contemporary culture" (Couldry, 2000b: 1). Let us, for now, take that as a given.

Cultural studies has many origins, and it is not part of my argument to fix upon one "origin" as primary (cf. Wright, 1998). Important to many of its starting points and explicit in the inspirational writing of one of its recognized sources, Raymond Williams, were two separate but related values, the first methodological and the second political. These two values can still orient us now. Cultural studies' *methodological* value derives from Williams's basic principle of avoiding language that massifies others (Williams, 1958: 306). As I put it in *Inside Culture,* echoing Williams: "We cannot oversimplify the cultural experiences of others, without caricaturing our own. Cultural studies in this sense involves an ethic of reciprocity, a mutual practice of both speaking and listening, which is inextricably tied to taking seriously the complexity of cultures" (Couldry, 2000b: 5).

Cultural studies' *political* value is participatory democracy itself, or rather the possibility of contributing through knowledge and debate to the preconditions of a genuine democracy of that sort. It is easy to forget that Raymond Williams's early writings emerged as part of a fierce *critique* of the failures of British democracy. For Williams, genuine democracy could never develop in the future without a "common culture," but this did not involve any naïve belief in consensus, quite the contrary: "A culture in common, in our own day, will not be the simple all-in-all society of old dream. It will be a very complex organisation, requiring continual adjustment and redrawing … this … difficulty is only soluble in a context of material community and by the full democratic process" (Williams, 1958: 318). Although Williams is sometimes dismissed for romanticizing "community," his insights into its uncertainty and democracy's fragility remain important.

In searching for a discipline that could do justice to the gap between people's personal experience and academic languages, Williams envisaged cultural studies as an account of contemporary culture and politics that was sensitive precisely to the unevenness of representation in established democracies like Britain. Getting social and cultural description *right* meant listening out for the complexities and varieties of voice, the inequalities of resource and position from which people spoke. This is what Williams meant by calling on us to abandon the "long dominative mode" (1961: 321) of thinking about culture. Old reifications, such as "mass culture" discourse, had to be abandoned and a more subtle form of cultural description developed. We will return to the question of experience below, but for now let's hold onto Williams's idea that there should be a fit between the way we think about the type of society we want—fractured space of elites and masses, or open space of equal citizens?—and the types of "knowledge" about society we produce, especially the degree to which we take account of the variability of voice.

The link from academic research to the conditions of democracy might seem a strange connection. It certainly contradicts the classic social science view that there is no place for explicit politics in academic research ("The prophet and the demagogue do not belong on the academic platform" [Weber, 1991b: 146]). But Williams's position fitted well with the shift toward a critical sociology that from the late 1950s onward was explicitly oriented toward the analysis of power (Mills, 1961; Gouldner, 1962). There is also an echo of the arguments of U.S. pragmatist philosopher and political theorist, John Dewey. Dewey, after World War I, argued that mass communications both transformed U.S. democracy and placed it in crisis (1946 [1927]: 126). The root of the crisis was not mistrust in political institutions, but cognitive dissonance: "Political apathy, which is a natural product of the discrepancies between actual practices and traditional machinery, ensues from [the] inability to identify one's self with definite issues. These are hard to find and locate in the vast complexities of current life" (1946: 134–135).

Not only could people not identify issues, but the "public" was too vast and fractured for any citizen to have a clear sense of what his or her membership of the public meant: "It is not that there is no public ... having a common interest in the consequences of social transactions. There is *too much public*, a public too diffused and scattered and too intricate in composition" (Dewey 1946: 137, added emphasis). For Dewey, the answer to the crisis of democracy was more democracy across all walks of life, including family, work, and education (1946: 143). For this, Dewey argued "free social inquiry" or social research was needed (1946: 163–180). It was left to Williams, however, to develop explicitly the idea that there might be a particular way of researching the social world that could better embody Dewey's ideal of democracy as "community life" (1946: 148).

Dewey's vision for reviving democracy seems old-fashioned in its reliance, as sole reference point, on the face-to-face community (Barnett 2003: chapters one and two). While we dismiss the importance of face-to-face experience at our peril, we equally know contemporary life involves such an interlocking of scales that it is, inevitably, in part mediated. The exclusively face-to-face community is hardly plausible in fact, let alone as ideal. The process whereby public issues and social groups are represented and mediated is one about which cultural studies cannot be unreflexive. Here is Stuart Hall on the apparently innocent notion of "popular culture": "Popular culture ... is not at all, as we sometimes think of it, the arena where we find who we really are, the truth of our experience. It is an area that is profoundly mythic.... It is there that we discover and play with the identifications of ourselves, where we are imagined, where we are represented" (1992: 22). Built into cultural studies, then, is a concern with the mechanisms of how we are represented.

This concern—traceable back at least to Williams—with what we would call now the "politics" of representation anticipates poststructuralist concerns with what Deleuze once called "the indignity of speaking for others."[5]

The theme also runs right through the applications, at least, of Derrida's philosophy of deconstruction (which, although originally focused primarily on relations between texts, was available also to deconstruct the rhetorical claims of the texts through which others were represented). Deconstruction's suspicion toward rhetoric was a useful tool in postcolonialism's challenge to hegemonic discourses of "race" and "nation" (Gilroy, 2000; Bhabha, 1994) and in postmodern ethnography's deconstruction of anthropology's colonial "authority" to represent distant others (Clifford, 1990). The "ethics" of deconstruction, which resonates well beyond debates about Derrida's texts, has its source in many places, not just in Derrida.

In fact, the ethics of representation is now so pervasive a concern in public culture and everyday life that it is hardly distinctive of cultural studies, or any other discipline. But new forms of the problem keep emerging: if identity was once an important term in resisting others' strategies to make one invisible, the term *identity* itself has validly been criticized for carrying with it a very limiting politics of representation. In a book whose original French title was *Les Identités Meurtrières* (Murderous Identities), Amin Maalouf, an Arab Christian from Lebanon now living in exile in France, eloquently contests the official badge of identity that "presupposes that 'deep down inside' everyone there is just one affiliation that really matters, a kind of 'fundamental truth' about each individual.... As if the rest, all the rest—a person's whole journey through time as a free agent; the beliefs he acquires in the course of that journey; his own individual tastes, sensibilities and affinities; in short his life itself—counted for nothing" (Maalouf, 2000: 4).

Yet, even if we recognize this complexity abstractly, Maalouf suggests, we proceed to ignore it in practice: we generally "behave as if it were not true. Taking the line of least resistance, we lump the most different people together under the same heading" (2000: 18). Implementing what I once called a "two-way principle of accountability" (Couldry, 2000b: 127) between our accounts of others and our accounts of ourselves is surprisingly hard in practice. We might speculate as to the reasons: one must lie in the necessity of any rhetoric running beyond itself (De Man, 1971); another may lie in the identitarian pressures in many contexts to shore up a sense of "self" by reifying the "other" against which it is defined (Benjamin, 1998: 95). This is not a problem exclusive to large-scale media representations of others, but it cannot be avoided by them either, particularly during global conflict when "others" are continually represented by media as actual or potential enemies (Butler, 2004: xviii, 146–150).

Although the ethics of representation is inherent to any contemporary social science that claims to know the social world through empirical research, cultural studies, at least in Williams's formulation, is distinctive for the *explicit* link it makes from ethics back to politics. Cultural studies does not just claim to exercise ethical responsibility in its discourse; cultural studies claims to be a discourse, in part, *about* the processes by which "others" get represented and therefore to derive its research priorities from a concern with the broadest cultural conditions of democracy itself. Cultural studies offers a specific sense of what it means to apply the ethics of representation on many levels (methodological, theoretical, political). This is the point on which I want to build later in arguing for the particular "promise" of cultural studies in today's circumstances of global conflict.

Listening to "Experience"

Raymond Williams imagined cultural studies in Britain as a space where the experience of working class subjects, missing from dominant accounts of Britain's "democracy" in the 1950s, could be heard. Important though Williams's insight about class remains, this formulation of the representational task of cultural studies cannot any longer satisfy us, since it selects drastically from the dimensions of inequality along which experience is discriminated and weighted for significance: what about gender, ethnicity, sexuality, age? But Williams's fundamental point remains intact: that cultural studies' intent should be to provide a space within academic discourse where experience is registered, *the exclusion of which from official representations damages the viability of democracy itself.* We must not miss the general importance of this point by tying it to its English origins. The educationalist Brazilian Paulo Freire made a similar point in the context of postcolonial education in Latin America: "Studying is above all thinking about experience, and thinking about experience is the best way to think accurately" (1985: 3).

What experience should cultural studies now be registering? First, it is obvious that we cannot begin to address this question except by thinking on a global scale—not because everyone now moves on a global scale (that privilege is unevenly distributed, which is part of the issue), but because, at a time of global conflict, the world's heightened interdependence and vulnerability rightly dominates our thoughts. However, and wherever, we live, the risks that engulf each of us are partly global in scale (Beck, 1992). The result is a gap between experience and languages of self-description that can be seen paradoxically as a source for identity itself: "Identity is formed at the unstable point where the 'unspeakable' stories of subjectivity meet the narratives of history, of a culture" (Hall, 1997 [1987]: 135). Certainly, we cannot think usefully about identity without paying attention to those wider disjunctures, particularly those of current global politics.

At a time when the balance of world communications remains massively imbalanced toward one "pole" of the global conflict (that associated with the United States), the experience of those without easy identification with that pole must clearly be listened to by cultural studies: for example, Muslims in the West who are currently subject to a great deal of scrutinizing by the UK and U.S. governments for their "loyalty." This is not the only possibility, of course: what of the experience of those who are apparently part of the dominant "civilization" (Huntington, 1997), yet dissent from it? We can apply here Judith Butler's call for the importance of "politicizing *dis*identification, [the] experience of *misrecognition,* this uneasy sense of standing under a sign to which one does not belong" (1993: 219). When a narrow elite's "war on terror" casts such a long shadow over everyday lives across the world, recognizing disidentification becomes simultaneously an intellectual and political commitment.

These are, of course, two radically different experiences—being part of a large section of the world population that, de facto, is excluded involuntarily from identifying with the world's dominant economic, military, and symbolic power, on the one hand, and rejecting one's ascribed membership of the West (or at least some of its implications), on the other—but they are facets of the same multisided process. The latter experience (disidentification) is easy for disidentifiers, myself included, to grasp, but the former is very difficult for the same people to grasp sufficiently for mutual understanding. So the former experience is easily neglected (Maalouf, 2000: 99; Ganguly, 2001: 4, 21). Yet the *untranslatability* (or limited translatability) of the experience of being at the receiving end of Western domination (for decades and centuries, yes, but particularly intense in the world of global live media and potential mutual visibility) is a problem within Western democracies. It is a problem that cultural studies should be prepared to address by listening to voices from right across the social terrain—including (and here we must remember cultural studies' commitment to studying "ordinary" culture) terrain that is easily neglected as "known in advance": the possibly conflicted, and surely complex, identifications and intuitions about "community" of, for example, the UK white majority. What places does respect for difference (ethnic, cultural, religious) have in people's understandings of themselves as British? If intuitions about the value of diversity exist, what sites are there for people to enact them or link them with the similar intuitions of others, apart from ritual moments (such as the extensively mediated two-minute silence in Europe one week after the July 2005 London bombings)?

Working through in the aftermath of the July 7 London bombings people's varying experiences of identity and difference will surely test the degree to which Britain is an effective democracy. Early press rhetoric, which puzzles over the conflict in the bombers between unquestionable "evil" and surface "ordinariness," promises little insight.[6] All democracies face the challenge of confronting their exclusions, and how well they do this tells us something about the extent to which they are genuinely democratic.

Etienne Balibar, considering the future of politics in a multiethnic Europe of porous borders puts this well: "The idea that I would like to defend is that *it is always the practical confrontation with the different modalities of exclusion* (social, and thus political, for the two notions have never truly been separate) *that constitutes the founding moment of citizenship*, and thus of its periodic test of truth" (Balibar 2004: 76, original emphasis). If cultural studies shares this concern with the preconditions of democracy, it must recognize the voices of those on the "margins" of the Western democratic pact and offer a site of dialogue with them.

Cultural Studies in Dangerous Times

Cultural studies places a value on representing the social world in terms that are adequate to the complexity each of us would want accorded to ourselves; and it values the ideals (we are far from the practice, as yet) of a democracy whose institutions embody respect for each citizen's voice in the management of common problems. Together, we might say, these two values amount to an ethics of cultural studies. But with global conflict intensifying, we need more than abstract values; our ethics must have a practical dimension if cultural studies is to redeem its promise in times of danger.

How can cultural studies do this? First, by recognizing that its values imply a practice of open, reflexive communication that is not an incidental luxury but a *necessity*, not a detour from politics but the *substance* of politics (or at least a precondition for that substance: "the politics of politics" as Balibar calls it). From outside cultural studies, Susan Buck-Morss argued in the wake of the September 11 attacks on New York and Washington that "what is needed is to rethink the entire project of politics within the changed conditions of a global public sphere—and to do this democratically, as people who speak different political languages, but whose goals are nonetheless the same: global peace, economic justice, legal equality, democratic participation, individual freedom, mutual respect" (Buck-Morss, 2003: 4–5).

For this we need produce "solidarity beyond and across the discursive terrains that determine our present collective identifications" (2003: 4). This requires more than talk; we need to change the conditions under which we communicate, in "the slow and painful task of a radically open communication that does not presume that we already know where we stand" (2003: 6). In this process of open communication, political languages on either side(s) of the global conflict need to be "mutually open to transformation" (2003: 7). This implies—which perhaps is where cultural studies can make a special contribution—hearing the subtle connections and disconnections between individual voices and the large forms of "political language." To those who say that a global "war on terror" requires us to focus on "our side" and its resources, not the exchange of ideas with "the other side," I cannot better Buck-Morss's response: "Nothing could be further from the truth. Terrorism will disappear because nonviolent ways of communication and debate are possible" (2003: 15).

But the principle of "open communication" will be insufficient unless we acknowledge one fundamental obstacle to dialogue: the automatic assumption of a secular framework. Certainly, I am secular in my outlook; in fact, my complete lack of religious beliefs is one of the few things I would recognize as unambiguously identifying me! I also work within social science and cultural studies, disciplines like many others that are based in an entirely taken-for-granted secularism. I do not want to give up, or undermine, my secularism. But that is different from insisting on an *assumption* of secularism as the only *possible* starting point for engagement with the questions that concern us in social science, cultural studies, and democratic reform.

Indeed, I want to question the usefulness of that assumption for a world whose major conflicts are presented, at least, in terms of conflicts between religions (I would not for one moment say that is how we should analyze them; but it is the representations that count). If we are serious about opening up our political language to transformation, then an essential step is to open up for discussion and criticism our own assumptions, too: to be ready, for a moment and in the interest of expanded, yet necessary dialogue, to place our values of secularism to one side in order to create the space for listening to others who start from a different position. Obviously, this will be an ineffective gesture, if in return we are faced with a complete unwillingness to listen to *our* position as people committed to secularism, and here I freely admit that things may stand very differently in the United Kingdom (with weak religious institutions) than in the United States (with financially and politically powerful religious institutions). Even so, we must recognize that being willing, temporarily, to put a fundamental assumption to one side in the interest of achieving dialogue that otherwise would be difficult is to recognize an even more fundamental principle than secularism: the hospitality required of everyone who must share the crowded surface of the earth. Kant, in his "philosophical sketch" on "perpetual peace," wrote of a basic "right to visit": "[a right to] associate, [that] belongs to all men by virtue of their common ownership of the earth's surface; for since the earth is a globe, they cannot scatter themselves infinitely, but must, finally, tolerate living in close proximity" (Kant, 1983 [1795]: 118).

As today's "ethnoscapes" (Appadurai, 1990) become ever more complex and intermixed, the principle of hospitality becomes all the more relevant. It implies a "linguistic hospitality" (Ricoeur, 1995) that must be reflected in the structure, not just the surface, of debate. We need new forms of exchange that acknowledge nonsecular voices *within* the space of cultural studies itself (not merely as an "other" to be managed along its boundary); the result, I believe, will be to strengthen, not weaken, the basis on which we can continue to argue *for* the values of secularism. For the requirement to listen to the voices of others is precisely a value of effective democracy itself, *provided* we face honestly the necessity to live with others who start from different positions from us and motivated by values we may not share.

Of course, these may be a problematic move to make in practice; it is foolish to ignore the difficulties. It may be helpful to acknowledge one problem that is *common* to all of us, whether secular or religious: how can the preconditions of democracy, indeed of peaceful coexistence, be thought about coherently when they are threatened by forces operating on a scale that far exceeds any scale on which we can act? I mean the "forces" behind both the U.S.–UK intervention in Iraq and the U.S. illiberal policy of dealing with those who are suspected of being threats to its security at Guantanamo Bay and elsewhere. Dewey, if we remember, suggested that apathy resulted from such a mismatch of scale, but this sense of inadequacy need not be impotent if we grasp it as a common problem *shared* by secularists and religious believers alike. Here George Marcus's principle of "complicity" (developed in an attempt to move "postmodern ethnography" beyond a spiraling concern for the impossibility of inauthenticity in fieldwork) may help. Let's listen to how Marcus carves out a possibility not of consensus but of exchange from what might otherwise be seen as an impasse between researcher and research subject: "[Complicity is] an awareness of existential *doubleness* on the part of both anthropologist and subject; this derives from having a sense of being *here* where major transformations are under way that are tied to things happening simultaneously *elsewhere*, but not a certainty or authoritative representation of what those connections are" (Marcus 1999: 97, original emphasis).

Shared complicity in the uncertainties and indeterminacies of the current world situation, and the conflicts of identification it throws up, may be a good starting point for open dialogue.

Conclusion

The promise of cultural studies has, I suggest, only begun to be redeemed. The current global conflict stimulates us to think what that promise might mean when not only the preconditions of democracy but also the most basic conditions of peaceful coexistence are under threat, not least from governments that go to war in unstable parts of the world without popular consent or general legitimacy. Principles can be derived from cultural studies' past, but they need to be refashioned for the challenges of the present. One such principle is the idea of "common culture" that, Raymond Williams argued, "we need ... not for the sake of an abstraction, but because we shall not survive without it" (1958: 304). If that concept is no longer available to us, we need to understand why; if it is available to us, but on altered terms, we need to understand how those terms help us think about the current state of democratic politics and cultural studies' relation to it. This is the task of the next chapter.

Notes

1. Couldry (2000b).

2. For an analogous link between the scientific concern with communication and the principle of participatory democracy, see Williams (1961: 118).

3. I say "mischievously" because Norris's reference point is Derrida's search for ethics through the deconstruction of the limits of the Western philosophical tradition, above all its notion of "reason." As we will see in chapter 7, I aim by contrast to draw on that tradition, not think "beyond" it. However, I do so by returning to Aristotle, rather than Plato or Kant; and it is the latter two, much more than Aristotle, that have been primary targets of Derrida's deconstruction. Indeed, Plato and Kant are as much rejected by those who broadly follow the line of thought from Aristotle in moral philosophy as they have been by Derrida—for example, Bernard Williams, whose 1985 book *Ethics and the Limits of Philosophy* has a title that strikingly, if perhaps unwittingly, echoes Derrida and Norris's reading of Derrida. At the same time my borrowing of the term *deconstruction* aims to convey a great respect for the analytic tools of deconstruction and their usefulness in undermining some of the myths and rhetorical sleights of our time: for an important and clear account of the implications of Derrida's work for communication theory, see Chang (1996).

4. Williams (1958: 320); Spivak (1990: 59); hooks (1994: 86).

5. In the conversation with Foucault, "Intellectuals and Power," reprinted in Foucault (1977: 209).

6. Cf. Butler (2004: 146) on images of "evil" enemies that undermine, not help, understanding.

5
In the Place of a Common Culture, What?

⊸

> We must set the idea of a "community of citizens" back in motion, in such
> a way that it should be the result of the contribution of all those who are
> present and active in the social space.
>
> —Balibar 2004: 50

The traditional notion of "community" rests on a close mapping of two
things: the times and spaces where we live, and our sense (both cognitive
and emotional) of commonality, of connection. But for all of us, even if in
different ways and to different degrees, those things are being pulled apart.
If you have lived, as I have, in an even moderately busy urban street, it makes
sense, although a weird kind of sense, that you do *not* speak to the person
who lives two doors down from you, who tends to go to work at the same
time as you, even if (as in one bizarre case that happened to me) it turns out
that person ends his or her journey to work only a few yards from where you
do! On the other hand, it makes sense to show significant pleasure, when
at a conference you meet only for the second time someone from a distant
university with whom (apart from broad outlines of work specialization)
your life and its milieu may have very little in common. So there are good
and bad sides, as always, to the stretching of time-space relations! But one
effect is that any particular milieu is characterized by what the sociologist
Martin Albrow has called "time-space social stratification" (1997: 52): our
paths move in parallel with those of countless others we rarely see, so that,
even when our paths do cross with theirs, the encounter may seem random
rather than meaningful.[1]

There is good reason, then, to loosen the tie between community and any defined geographical area and, as Gerard Delanty (2003) argues in his useful recent survey of the term, to allow for "communication communities" that stretch in many forms across territorial boundaries. To hold onto the assumption that community is based, at a minimum, on the grouping of people in *one* place (as recently the *Penguin Encyclopaedia of Sociology* still did: Abercrombie et al., 2000) is to condemn our definition to irrelevance. But the opposite is not true: relaxing our definition of community in this way does not guarantee its relevance, or not, at least, if it is relevance to politics we want. The term *politics* is itself subject to continuous redefinition within debates over global human rights and cosmopolitanism.[2] But, however we stretch and relayer our concept of *politics*, the term is unimaginable without some meshing between, on the one hand, the "places" where we live, work, and are governed and, on the other hand, the places where we share with others something that impinges on how we are governed, something that might provide the matter of politics. For, as Chantal Mouffe in her book *The Democratic Paradox* has argued, "The logic of democracy does indeed imply a moment of closure which is required by the very process of constituting 'the people' [which] cannot be avoided," even if from a philosophical perspective we might now insist on the paradoxical nature of that closure (Mouffe, 2000: 43). Democratic politics, Mouffe argues, drawing on Wittgenstein, requires some "form of life," that is, a *sufficient* level of shared beliefs and "practice … aimed at persuading people to broaden the range of their commitments to others, to build a more inclusive community" (2000: 65–66). Mouffe's use of the term *community* is striking, even surprising, in the deconstructionist context of her book, but the fact that she is driven to use it illustrates precisely the tension I now want to explore.

The Problematic "Place" of the Political (A Philosophical Detour)

This tension has troubled me in my own work on culture and media for some time. I mean the conflict between two apparently irreconcilable pressures: on the one hand, the push to root out and deconstruct any notions of "unity" or "holism" lurking behind the everyday political language of "society," "state," "culture," and "community" (not least in their media glosses)[3] and, on the other hand, the pull back toward *some* notion of commonality without which any refounding of democratic politics seems impossible, even unimaginable. Where can we turn for the language, the concepts, the practices that might express this commonality without unity?[4] Before I go any further, let me acknowledge that to put things this way—to foreground the *preconditions* of political engagement—might seem, to some, an intolerable diversion, if the ultimate goal is to link back to politics itself. But it is a step that I believe is necessary, and one that cultural studies has an important role in helping us formulate effectively; it may be, as Balibar argues, an essential step if we are to "set the idea of a 'community of citizens' back in motion." I return to politics as such at the end of the chapter.

Taken at face value (although as we saw in the last chapter Williams's actual language leaves more room for complexity), the terms in Raymond Williams's well-worn notion of *common culture* seem unusable for resolving the tension I have outlined: *common,* because it assumes something held in common that we can no longer assume; and *culture,* because of its reliance on the interpretive closure of long-deconstructed metaphors.[5] But that does not mean we can abandon the *conceptual site* that Williams intended the term *common culture* to mark, which is why this chapter's title tries to keep that site open. We can at least hope that some new term might come to reoccupy this place; without this, Williams was right to say that "we shall not survive" (1958: 304), or at least a genuine democratic politics will not survive.

How can this conceptual site be characterized? Mouffe writes of a contestatory democracy formed of "friendly enemies," "who are friends because they share a common symbolic space" (2000: 13). But she does not hint how that common symbolic space might be created or sustained. This gap in her argument is symptomatic; it is common to both political science and political theory. We might hope for solutions in the fast-growing literature on citizenship, but for all its richness there is, as yet, as Thomas Janoski and Brian Gras (2002: 42) recently pointed out, nothing there that captures "the informal aspects of citizenship *integrating* both the public and private sphere," precisely the gap between life world and public connection with which I began. Instead, the value of citizenship studies may lie in the nakedness of the questions it asks: "What does it mean to belong to society?" (Stevenson, 2002: 4); "What counts as community and solidarity?" (Elliott, 2002: 55).

While such unanswered questions confirm the existence of a gap, I would want to go further and interpret this gap as symptomatic of a crisis in the practice of democracy itself, a crisis quite consistent with the survival (for now at least) of democratic values.[6] This is partly a crisis in the dominant liberal model of democracy, which, as its critics (Pateman, 1970; Barber, 1984) have long argued, is a thin concept of democracy, fully compatible with a permanently disengaged minority, but less easily compatible with a disengaged *majority* (Wolin, 1992). But the crisis goes wider; it is a problem for all who want to work with an older language of politics that has been stretched beyond all recognition by the competing forces of detraditionalization, individualization, and globalization. As a result, the crisis applies equally to radical versions of democratic politics. Let me illustrate this by surveying, quite critically, some recent, mainly philosophical, interventions in the redefinition of *politics,* or at least of the preconditions of political engagement.

Jacques Derrida has provided, perhaps, the most vivid image of the democratic crisis itself. In *Politics of Friendship,* he writes of how "the resonant echo of all the great [political] discourse" now issues, increasingly, in "mad and impossible pleas, almost speechless warnings." These warnings turn endlessly "like searchlights without a coast, they sweep across the dark sky, shut down or disappear at regular intervals and harbour the invisible in their very light" (Derrida, 1997: 81). For Derrida, the problem is a crisis in the nature of value itself, in "the value of value." This cannot be addressed through some reworked democratic bond based on community, or "fraternity," in any substantive sense, because it is the unsustainability of such political "substances" that is the problem. Instead, Derrida recalls Aristotle's concept of "friendship," but with a sense, derived from Blanchot, of mutual strangeness and separation (Derrida, 1997: 294). But what contexts, what reference points does Derrida give us for thinking about this new politics, and how it might be sustained? Apart from an enigmatic mention of "a certain faithful memory of democratic reason and reason *tout court"* (1997: 306), there is no clue.

Nor, although many have turned to it for guidance, does the philosophy of Levinas provide, I would argue, many hints as to how we might sustain, let alone extend, its rethinking of morality into social practice and the possible refounding of politics. The unconditional, asymmetrical responsibility that Levinas argues we have toward the Other who faces us is *prior* to any social or cultural process; it is built into the prior constitution of the self. As Zygmunt Bauman puts it in his eloquent book *Postmodern Ethics,* "It is through stretching myself towards the Other that I have become the unique, the only, the irreplaceable self that I am" (1992: 77). But how is this abstract vision of morality, which rejects any basis in something as contingent as consensus or mutuality, connectable to the progressive "remoralization of human space" for which Bauman calls (1992: 249, 250)?[7] It is far from obvious.

Something of the same impasse affects Jean-Luc Nancy's evocation of "the inoperative community" (1991). This community is inoperative in the sense that it is sustained only through the *absence* of the rhetorical operations of reification, on which conventional notions of community depend: "It is the work that the community does *not* do and it is *not* that forms community ... Community is made of what retreats from it" (1991: xxxix). Like Levinas, Nancy turns to the original constitution of the self for value: our prior sense of "being-in-common" with others, which is indissolubly tied to our knowledge of our and their mortality. We should be wary of exaggerating the novelty of these formulations; the insistence on the necessary intersubjectivity of the self goes back at least to the 1930s U.S. pragmatist George Herbert Mead.[8] What is new here, however, beyond the elegantly paradoxical language, is not obviously helpful. For, by contrast with U.S. pragmatists like Mead and Dewey, who connected philosophical issues to the social and cultural bases of democratic education and politics, Nancy seems to turn his back on this: "Community," he writes, "is the *unworking* of work that is social, economic, technical and institutional" (1991: 31, added emphasis). "Community," for Nancy, is something to be explored in the experience of seeing a friend die or in the philosophical foundations of literature, but not in anything that might readily be recognized as politics. Only one clue is offered, when Nancy addresses the word *political* itself: "*Political* would mean a community ordering itself to the unworking of its communication, or destined to this unworking: community consciously undergoing the experience of its sharing ... undergoing, in whatever manner, the experience of community as communication" (1991: 40–41).

Once again, there is an echo of pragmatism: recall John Dewey's definition of *communication* as "the way in which people come to possess things in common" (quoted Carey, 1989: 22). Nancy's idea, however, of a community that undermines, rather than simply sustains, its own "unity" (cf. Balibar, 2004: 76) is an important one to which I return.

For a less paradoxical account of the potential commonality that might ground any new politics, we can turn to work influenced by psychoanalytic conceptions of the self, not just in France but in Germany, Italy, and the United States. Kristeva's proposal that we be more open to strangers by becoming "strangers to ourselves" (1991) is well known, but similar connections between a more inclusive politics and the interrogation of the self have been developed by Axel Honneth (1995) and Jessica Benjamin (1998). It is a powerful line of argument, since it confronts the intense investment in *exclusion* that, whether or not we think within a psychoanalytic framework, is plausibly central to the constitution of the subject. Alessandro Ferrara (1998) has gone further and argued that psychoanalytic insights into the healthy subject can provide an intuitive basis for a new vision of "the good," which translates Aristotle's species-based notion of the "good for man" into a shared, but always individually worked out, value found in the richness of the life narrative. I will draw in detail on neo-Aristotelian approaches to the "good" in chapter 7. One problem, however, with Ferrara's argument is that psychoanalytic perspectives on the self are themselves normalizing; they are based implicitly on a standard of the healthy, fulfilled self, which is hardly consensual, and that I, for one, would want to contest.[9]

These psychoanalytic accounts, however, represent a major step forward away from the abstractions of the "originary constitution of the self" to questions of *process*—the processes, including narrative processes, through which selves emerge and evolve their reflexive understanding. This connects with the political sociologist Alain Touraine's (2000) attempt to transvalue the standard terms of democratic discourse (*freedom, solidarity, equality*) for a world where the nation as a founding "essence" is neither desirable nor plausible. We have already seen in chapter 2 the context for this shift, in terms of many social theorists' scepticism about classic sociology's assumption of the national "society" as a container for social action; here we see the problem that this scepticism may cause for political theory. The way forward, Touraine argues, is through a new attention to the *Subject*: "We have to replace the old idea of democracy, defined as participation in the general will, with the new idea of institutions that safeguard the freedom of the Subject and permit communication between Subjects" (2000: 14). By *subject*, Touraine means any individual subject, but what might these communicative institutions be? Or, more modestly, on what principles can they even be imagined? Once again, we are offered few clues by Touraine beyond this general statement.

The only writer whom I have found to offer a way forward here is the philosopher and narrative theorist, Paul Ricoeur. For Ricoeur, the self is always a narrated self: the self subsists through the never-completed stories it tells of itself. Indeed, my individual story can never be sealed off from the stories others tell of themselves: "The life history of each of us is caught up in the histories of others" (Ricoeur, 1992: 161). This means that, in principle, each of us is disposed to be interested in the stories of others. What blocks a more open narrative exchange, Ricoeur argues, is the rigidity of collective identity, its tie to a founding event that must be kept unchanged, indeed "incommunicable," to perform its political work (Ricoeur 1995: 7, quoted in Kaplan, 2003: 97). In rejecting the closure underlying collective identities, Ricoeur follows all the other writers I have discussed, but crucially he goes further in suggesting some specific *practices* that might allow us to move beyond such unsatisfactory identities. One is what Ricoeur calls a "translation ethos" (or "language of hospitality"), that is, an openness to each other's narrative languages. Another is the "exchange of memories" that offers conflicting accounts of overlapping events. We need, Ricoeur implies, institutions where, across apparent differences of collective identity, we can exchange narratives of past experience that, through their exchange, encourage shared narratives of the future.[10]

All this might seem to take us very far from sociology! But, as Touraine points out, if the crisis of democratic values runs as deep as many, including him, suggest, we cannot go on describing the social and political world as if nothing is changing. The very purpose of critical social analysis itself is at stake (2000: 11; cf. Honneth, 1995: 207). Cultural studies, as we saw in chapter 4, is distinguished by having made this link between democratic conditions and social inquiry explicit.

So, to sum up my argument, we need a language and a practice (or form of life) that can connect *across* our anxious cross-disciplinary searches: first, for the regrounding of ethics and morality; second, for new models of democratic politics; and, third, for new analytic concepts for critically understanding the social world. In this spirit, I want to ask what contribution cultural studies might make to developing that common language and practice.

Researching the Spaces of Everyday Politics

Right away, let me stress that I have no illusions that cultural studies, more than any other academic subject, carries some automatic political force (there is no role now, as Bauman [1987] pointed out, for academic "legislators"; so an academic subject's political "force" must be generated through the specific and practical connections it makes to the world beyond it). Nor do I have too many illusions about the difficulties that the intensified rationalization of contemporary academic life poses for such a political practice: we should not forget that the original Centre for Contemporary Cultural Research at Birmingham University was closed down in the summer of 2002 because of just such pressures. Nor, given the wider problem, precisely, of *making connections* between specialized forms of life, does it make sense to speak as if research and teaching can be reformed in isolation from shifts in practices outside the academy. Academic principles matter little, unless opened to the wider democratic dialogue that in my book *Inside Culture* (2000b: 140) I tried to capture through the phrase "community without closure"—a phrase that was itself unspecific, I admit, but to which I want to try to give some substance here. More on that later.

Here, I need to argue for a research agenda for cultural studies that is rather different from its current one: this is intended not so much as a judgment on cultural studies' past as a proposal that, if cultural studies is to contribute more concretely to the crisis of democratic politics than some of the philosophical positions that I have criticized, it must change its priorities.

So how, given these qualifications, might we imagine the contribution of cultural studies? By *cultural studies,* I mean, since the question of cultural studies' disciplinary status seems permanently unresolved,[11] loosely the range of work across the social sciences and humanities that acknowledges the inspiration of cultural studies.

Let's start with two points. First, we must be realistic: such is the fragmentation of the intellectual public sphere, in Britain at least, and cultural studies' dispersed and largely marginal position within it, that no single intervention is ever likely to have the impact that Raymond Williams's book *Culture and Society* did in 1950s Britain. A more differentiated network of interventions is needed that is open in multiple ways to exchanges beyond conference hall and teaching room: in how cultural studies conceives the research work appropriate to it, in how it translates that research into writing and other interventions, in how it disseminates that research and feeds it into ideas for further research and wider nonacademic dialogue. It follows (and this is the second point) that it makes no sense for cultural studies to limit its questions to those that arise in an academic framework, ignoring the most urgent issues that face the social and political world, including the very crisis in democratic politics that I have been discussing.

Looking back to the situation faced by Raymond Williams, there is a striking parallel as well as enormous differences. Williams articulated better than most around him the coming democratic crisis in a postwar society rigidly stratified by class, a Britain far from achieving the "new common experience" that at the dawn of the welfare state T. H. Marshall (1992 [1949]: 33) had seen as central to a stable pact of citizenship. Marshall had used the terms *culture* and *common experience* in a cryptic way, but by forging those terms into the critical concept of *common culture*, Williams cut into the less than democratic languages and cultural politics of his day.

The crisis of democratic politics is far from over (hence the continuity with Williams), but the forms and conceptual tools through which it can be addressed are necessarily very different after five decades in which the landscape of capacities and experiences we call *culture* has been destratified in some respects and relentlessly individualized in others. The issue remains the building of connections to resist the fragmentation of the "world of discourse" (Williams, 1968: 133), but the divisions to be resisted are not so much the barriers of taste that differentiate types of cultural work from each other, but rather the divisions that block off the sites of possible politics from the rest of life (Bauman, 1999: 2).

There may now, in other words, be much less at stake in the general term *culture*, whose use, after all, has been endlessly expanded and whose political weight has been deconstructed to death (which is how I read the upshot of Tony Bennett's [1998] work); and much more at stake in the idea of "*common* culture," or at least (as I put it earlier) in the conceptual site that Williams intended to mark by that apparently defunct phrase. For what is urgent now is not defending the full range of cultural production and consumption from elitist judgment (an old story), but defending the possibility of *any* shared site (whether or not it overlaps with specialized spheres of cultural production) for an emergent democratic politics. The contemporary mission of cultural studies, if it has one, lies not with the study of culture (already a cliché of management and marketing manuals) but with the fate of a common culture and its contemporary deformations.

The Fate of Political Agency

There are many ways of developing this insight into specific research within cultural studies. One—perhaps the most direct, which is not to claim it is necessarily the best—is to look for new empirical routes into the problem of *the political*, as it is currently experienced and constructed; to examine how, from a host of different perspectives, the political is being constituted, reformed, and suppressed. Already there is work on the discourses of politics in circulation or, just as important, *not* in circulation: Engin Isin's Foucauldian work on the construction of citizenship, or Henry Giroux's and Loic Wacquant's analyses of the displacement in U.S. politics of issues of "race" and exclusion.[12] Or we could deconstruct the apparently innocent metaphors such as *community*, which provide cover for the work of refiguring and desocializing the language of government (Rose, 1996)—remember the motto of Huxley's *Brave New World:* "Community Identity Stability"! All such analyses need to be placed in the wider context of the growing hegemony of neoliberalism (Bourdieu, 1998; Giroux, 2004a).

I want here, however, simply because it is closer to my own style of research, to focus on work with political *subjects,* the agents, potentially, in political change (or in its absence). They are important, because in their reflexivity can be sensed the local rhetorical work to which *the political* and related terms are being put, and what, if anything, may still be at stake in these terms; they are important, more basically, because their very actions preserve the possibility of renewing the political.

In previous work, I analyzed practices on the very margins of the political by people with few, if any, media resources who receive little, if any, recognition for their political intent: the women who continued a life of protest at Yellow Gate around the Greenham Common U.S. Air Force Base until 2001 (Couldry, 1999), the "Umbrella Man" who through the 1990s and early 2000s has waged many individual campaigns on unfashionable issues such as trade union and disability rights (Couldry, 2001a).

We should be under no illusions about the generosity of the state toward those who challenge the boundaries of acceptable political action. If you have been near the British Houses of Parliament over the past five years, you will probably have seen Brian Haw who has lived outside the Palace of Westminster protesting the belligerent policies of the Blair New Labour government.[13] This is the same, symbolically important, space—outside the entrance to the center of British political power—that the Umbrella Man has often used to gain attention for his causes. But the freedom of movement and action that enable such protest was lost on August 1, 2005, when the UK's Serious Organised Crimes and Policing Act[14] came into force. Section 132 of that act imposes a general ban on organizing a public demonstration, or taking part in one, or even demonstrating alone, within "the designated area" (a one-kilometer radius from the edge of Parliament Square, the supposed symbolic center of Britain's democracy). The only exception is if the person has the prior consent of the metropolitan police commissioner, which requires a detailed written application at least twenty-four hours in advance. Even then, conditions can be imposed, for example, to present "disruption to the life of the community" (whatever *community* means in the streets of government buildings and corporate public relations offices that surround Westminster).

The details matter less than the legislative intent, which is clear enough: to remove forever the freedom of action (however limited) that made "tactics" like those of the Umbrella Man or Brian Haw possible within the "strategically" regulated space of British politics (de Certeau's [1984] distinction between "strategies" of power and "tactics" that operate within and across them, remains relevant). The protests against this illiberal legislation have already begun, but now they take place on pain of arrest and criminal charges.[15] Recall that this legislation was brought into force by the same government that just a month earlier had lavished praise during the buildup to the G8 Gleneagles Summit on the protests most closely associated with its own public relations machine (the Make Poverty History campaign)[16]—and you see that nothing is less "neutral" than the boundaries of legitimate political expression in this age of neoliberalism by spectacle.[17]

Politics and Everyday Life

Another approach to the experiential dimension of politics passes, not through political action (or its contested boundaries), but through everyday reflexivity about the public world. This is an area where, with my LSE colleagues Sonia Livingstone and Timothy Markham,[18] I have been working for the past two years on a project called "Media Consumption and the Future of Public Connection." This project is definitely *not* aimed at reinforcing the rigid assumptions about the place or nature of politics that characterize most political science. Rather, it has taken a broadly social constructionist[19] approach to politics, asking people who are not necessarily active in the formal political process for *their* reflections on where, if anywhere, a meaningful sphere of public issues lies beyond the private domain, and whether, if at all, media are involved in sustaining their orientation to that world.

There is no space to summarize the project's results here (for this, see Couldry, Livingstone, and Markham, forthcoming). Instead, I want to reflect, at least from my own perspective as someone interested in both media research and cultural studies,[20] on the *type* of research this has been and its implications for how we think about the future contribution of cultural studies to our understanding of the "politics of politics."

We knew in this project we would need to tread carefully. We would not have started it without some concern for the future of democratic politics, but we knew that as researchers we should avoid assuming we knew better than anyone else *where* and even *whether* politics has a future. "Where," because as Larry Grossberg argued in his unjustly neglected book *We Gotta Get Out of This Place:* "The analyst cannot assume that she or he already knows the proper locations at which people should invest themselves and construct their belongingness. Nor can he or she assume that the connections between such sites are always given in advance, so that people's travels through daily life are predictable" (1992: 110).

We cannot assume politics (in any recognizable sense) has a future because that would be to ignore the particular privilege of the researcher as knowledge producer (cf. Bourdieu, 2000) whose socially established role is precisely to elicit "opinions" about matters already constructed as important in advance from the vantage point of academic interpretation, whether or not they matter to the subjects of that research.[21] This is why the best empirical studies of political alienation and disconnection leave it ambiguous whether such positions are rational in the face of entrenched inequalities, including the fundamental political inequality between those who act (but may not listen) and those who (normally) are acted upon (Croteau, 1995; LeBlanc, 1999; Buckingham, 2000).[22]

In response, our approach has been to listen carefully—through multiple interviews, through focus groups, and most importantly, through the three-month diaries that our subjects wrote or spoke for us—to the reflections of those who are not, on the face of it, political agents, on what matters to them as significant beyond things of purely private significance, and what role media play in sustaining attention to that *public world* (however they define it). This is what we mean by researching public connection, rather than political engagement itself. Our concern—and here I believe it intersects with a core task of cultural studies—is with a crucial precondition of politics, as it is embedded in the patterns and constraints of everyday life (constraints of time, resources, status, purpose).

Institutional Cultures of Politics

Once again, however, this is just one possibility. Another would be to shift the focus away from individuals studied in the artificial situation of "pure" research, and toward the *institutional contexts* in which people and systems mobilize and negotiate the political (and that constitute its inclusions and exclusions). Cultural studies could do more, I suggest, to study institutional sites of discourse that are a long way from the formal process of politics, yet hardly divorced from questions of the political or community.[23] Hospitals and schools, for example, are sites of formal and voluntary work, and nodes in complex regulatory processes where class, educational, and ethnic differences as well as public resource strategies are daily negotiated. Potentially, therefore, they are sites of politics. How is that politics enacted in practice? Here the work directed by Phil Cohen at the UK's University of East London and Ien Ang at Australia's Centre for Cultural Research, University of Western Sydney, is unusual in taking seriously these openings for new types of *empirical* research in cultural studies.

Clearly, it cannot be enough to study those sites in isolation from the wider life trajectories of those who pass through them—because the political may be precisely what is excluded or marginalized in the sphere of "work" and many sites of leisure, too (cf. Eliasoph, 1999). This links with cultural studies' long-term respect for the individual voice (cf. Couldry, 2000b, chapters 3 and 7). To grasp how the possibilities for politics (in the sense of explicit collective negotiations) are controlled and managed, attention must be paid to politics in a different sense, the implied politics of speech or voice: the distribution, probably highly uneven, of people's sense (not necessarily directed to any space called politics) of themselves as effective agents and legitimate voices. Conventional political science has long traveled this coast in researching "civic culture" and "subjective efficacy" (Almond and Verba, 1963), but it has rarely gone far inland. We approach here the territory of "identity politics," usually discussed at the level of group allegiances. But in times when there is a problem even "of knowing what the speculative concept of community means" (Balibar, 2004: 65), we cannot limit our research to identities legitimated by group membership, unless we are prepared to ignore the space of individual uncertainty that lies beyond them. Nor, if we understand identities as, in a sense, "chosen," should we ignore how people's capacity to *choose* (or even their capacity to imagine themselves as agents who *might choose*) is shaped by fundamental material conditions such as the largely involuntary contexts of everyday work and family. This was brought home to me when, in a pilot for the "Public Connection" project, involving questions posed to the UK's Mass-Observation Archive Panel, a recently retired female nurse wrote in her response: "If my views counted for nothing after 50 years doing the job I knew about, why should they count about other things I know less about?"[24]

To be fair, these, as it were, subterranean connections between the crisis of formal politics and the undemocratic politics of work are beginning to be sensed within political science and political sociology (Bennett, 1998;

Turner, 2001); they were already registered in both Williams's and Dewey's calls for democratization right across the institutions of everyday life including the workplace (Williams, 1961; Dewey, 1946 [1927]: 143), but they have not so far generated much empirical research in cultural studies.[25]

Yet cultural studies, in the broad sense used here, has a great deal to contribute to such questions. This might sound a long way from some versions of cultural studies. Such an inquiry does not foreground cultural consumption or identity expression through cultural consumption; nor does it foreground processes of cultural production—not because they are unimportant (although, as I suggest, less may be directly at stake in these areas than once was the case), but because it aims to cut across those domains to foreground another set of questions about the intertwined fates of individual agency and democratic politics. In doing so, cultural studies is not ceding its territory to a revamped political sociology but, rather, bringing to an important interdisciplinary question (the preconditions of democratic politics) its interest in agency and voice and the forces that constrain them. In this way, cultural studies' long-standing allegiance to participatory democracy (cf. chapter 4) can become the direct *object* of cultural studies' research and teaching practice.

Cultural studies, of course, cannot work here on its own: the alliances it makes with other disciplines, on the face of it more directly concerned with the stuff of politics, are crucial. But before turning to that, first let me explain what I believe has to change in how cultural studies sees it own practice.

The Public Time of Cultural Studies

There are plenty of potential spaces for politics perhaps, but the key lack in the political domain may now be *time*, not space (Turner, 2002: 28). In a wonderful essay on the significance of rhetoric, the philosopher Hans Blumenberg wrote that "what has been designated in our tradition as 'rationality' has almost always benefited the element of acceleration … rhetoric, on the other hand, is, in regard to the temporal texture of actions, … a consummate embodiment of retardation" (1987: 444–445). As a result, "a disproportion has arisen between the acceleration of processes and the feasibility of keeping a 'feel' for them, of intervening in them with decisions, or coordinating them, through an overview, with other processes … [so that] there is something like the expediency of what is not expedient" (1987: 445–446).

Blumenberg here expresses in more general terms a suspicion toward the informational flows in contemporary life that is analogous to this book's reserve toward the media process: to listen beyond the echoes, we have to wait for them to die away! The specific resonance of Blumenberg's comment for the hyperrationalized world of the early twenty-first century workplace (of which universities are just one symptom) hardly needs elaboration.

Henry Giroux, in an eloquent lecture delivered ironically enough in that often complacent seat of ancient learning, Oxford University, posed a related question about what he called "public time": "How might public time, with its unsettling refusal to be fixed or to collapse in the face of corporate time, be used to create pedagogical conditions that foster forms of self and social critique as part of a broader project of constructing alternative desires and critical modes of thinking, on the one hand, and democratic agents of change, on the other?" (Giroux, 2004b: 160).

The notion of public time is a fascinating one because it captures many of the preconditions of democratic politics currently under threat: time to pay *attention*[26] (i.e., enough time to find out what we need to know about the world around us to grasp politics); time to *reflect* by ourselves and with others on the information we've acquired; and time to *deliberate* about what should be done. Time spent by individuals, particularly on the first two of these three, might be considered "private" time. But, if there is a clear public frame within which that private time is given meaning, then all those pockets of private time take on a new status as fragments of public time. By contrast, when the frame of public discourse undermines the idea that individual time spent reflecting on public matters is useful (or when it undermines the idea of political agency itself: Giroux, 2004a: xix), then individual time spent on political reflection and information gathering may seem empty, pointless.

Can cultural studies, then, through the dialogues that its research generates, aspire to be one fragment of that imagined, but perhaps threatened, public time? That is what I want to argue. What might this mean? First, that cultural studies should be a process in which people's fragmented, uncertain, incomplete narratives of agency (and all our narratives are inherently incomplete, as Ricoeur reminds us) can be valued, preserved, and made available for exchange, while being related, analytically, to wider contexts of power. Cultural studies could—a vision shared not just by Raymond Williams and Henry Giroux but by other figures as diverse as Judith Butler (2004) and Cornel West (1993)—contribute to sustaining dialogues that *bridge* the personal and the public, including debates about public culture that sustain the fragments of community embedded within it, while also being sharply critical, when necessary, of their contradictions and limitations. This is the process Henry Giroux calls "public pedagogy," intending it to apply well beyond the confines of academic institutions; indeed, it *must* extend into the less structured exchanges of civil society, if it is to have any meaning.[27]

We can draw here on Johannes Fabian's much older reflections on anthropology as a communicative process. Fabian (1983) argued that anthropology made a space of discourse for itself by constructing distant others as locked in a different, and subordinated, temporality. Yet time could play a different role, Fabian argued, in communication that was not exploitative: "For human communication to occur, coevalness has to be created. Communication is ultimately about shared time" (1983: 30–31), which is a mutually acknowledged and common frame of action. But, as Fabian also pointed out, *shared time* is a complex construction, "socially embedded in culturally organised praxis" (1983: 34). Cultural studies cannot hope to contribute to a revival of democratic politics unless it is involved on a practical level in the construction of shared time in this sense.

This must involve, in part, what Ricoeur (1995) calls "linguistic hospitality," providing a threshold for the exchange of memories and narratives by self and others. It would involve listening, as Ricoeur emphasizes, across difference, but on this point we can also go back to Raymond Williams, recalling what he says in *Culture and Society:* "Wherever we have started from, we need to listen to others who have started from a different position" (1958: 320). But it would be a process that made no claims to negate difference through false aspirations to completion or certainty. Remember how Raymond Williams sought to replace the false closures of mass-culture thinking with a new uncertainty in cultural discourse: "To the degree that we find [that] formula [of 'the mass'] inadequate for ourselves, we can wish to extend to others the courtesy of acknowledging *the unknown*" (1958: 289, added emphasis).[28]

The public time of cultural studies would, of course, from one point of view—that of rationalization and government managerialism—be "inexpedient" (Blumenberg's word). It would be a process that was "inoperative" in Jean-Luc Nancy's sense, undoing the false work of discourses that seek to construct "a unique and ultimate identity" out of the potential openness of communication (Nancy, 1991: xxxviii), working against the sanctioned languages of "people," "nation," "society," "culture," and even "identity" (cf. Balibar, 2004: 76). As such, it would enact Nancy's enigmatic words about "a community ordering itself to the *unworking* of its communication" while at the same time, and through that very process, "consciously undergoing the experience of its sharing" (Nancy, 1991: 40). Central to its work must be the unworking of the myths (tied closely to certain ideas of "nation" and "community") that pass for the substance of politics. There is a path here back to the work I have done on media rituals (Couldry, 2003a) since media institutions provide a key infrastructure for contemporary social rhetoric, including in the arena of politics.

None of this, however, would matter much if, as a research practice, it were not itself embedded effectively within a sphere of public action. It is here we confront the crux between the forward-looking work, say, of Paul

Ricoeur and the pessimism of Hannah Arendt. Arendt, from a conservative perspective—but that does not, as Michael Warner (2002: 59) points out, make her insight any less powerful—saw in modernity "the loss of the public realm" (1958: 55): the loss, that is, of an ensured space of public significance where individuals can make sense of sacrificing their private time in order to speak to, and act in view of, others. Not that contemporary phenomena such as reality television don't simulate such a space, which is precisely why they need to be deconstructed. Arendt's pessimism is perhaps a more useful starting point than Habermas's normative concept of the public sphere precisely because Arendt foregrounds the problematic nature of the links between private life and the public realm (this is why I have ignored public sphere debates so far, important though they may be for other purposes; for further discussion see chapter 7). Even so, Arendt's pessimism should not stop cultural studies from attempting connections beyond theory, within the world of politics itself even if, when formal politics is so dominated by the "war on terror," it is difficult to see an entry point for other voices. Let's turn to this problematic connection to politics in the chapter's final section.

The Space of Civility

Imagining in theory the preconditions for a renewed politics tells us nothing about whether life contexts exist in which such a politics might take root as practice. Practice is where real agents, formed and operating under major constraints but always with a local sense of possibility, choose what to do with their scarce resources including time; what, we might ask, can theories of narrative exchange and "inoperative community" tell us about the choices that people in fact make?

The problem with individualization and connected processes of desocialization (Touraine, 2000) that have undermined older social contexts, institutional and communal, is not that the social world has become drained of meaning (a lack for theorists to "fill in"), but that it is saturated by personal and public meanings whose trajectory, however, is more and more difficult to *connect* into any shared space of public action.[29] *True* public space may, in other words, be as scarce as public time (Kaiser 2003, quoted by Giroux, forthcoming, a). The fear, derived from Arendt, that the public realm may no longer be compatible with the way we now live, even if for a while it remains imaginable by theorists, is summed up by Oscar Gandy with nightmarish clarity when he writes that "the aura of personalization that surrounds new media" now means that "individuals may actually feel better about knowing less and less about the world around them" (Gandy, 2002: 452). For Gandy (cf. Sunstein, 2000), the very fabric of the public world is wearing thin, as even media consumption loses its implications of being part of public space/time and becomes, instead, merely an optional personal "download." What if, for this reason, all cultural studies' sophisticated proposals of mutual understanding and dialogue feed into, rather than challenge, this fragmentation? Can we say with confidence at what point does cultural studies' practice move from being an option for private study to becoming a practice within public space and time? The concept of public time challenges us to reconsider the parameters of today's educational experience and the cultural work it does (for a valuable treatment of these questions in intercultural settings, see Tanaka, 2003).

Raising these questions about the status of cultural studies as a social practice generates many more questions. Some concern university life and the increasing dominance of accountancy-driven managerialism (see Giroux and Giroux, 2004). Others relate to the wider public world and politics. Let me concentrate on the latter set of questions.

First, I want to answer the objection anticipated earlier that to spend so much time as I have considering the preconditions of politics is a diversion from what should be the real matter in hand: politics itself. I have some sympathy with this: I have no liking for the politics of academic writing that treats the sustaining of its own (relatively) privileged voice as a substitute for political action. But we must also be wary of being too impatient here. It is striking that the historic public realm Arendt describes as lost, perhaps irrevocably, shares one feature with the community that other thinkers from Williams to Nancy have been trying to envisage—for the future. The essential feature of the public realm is its "publicity." *Publicity* in Arendt's sense, even if couched in an older language, shares something important with those more forward-looking visions. Here is Arendt: "Being seen and being heard by others derive their significance from the fact that everybody sees and hears *from a different position*. This is the meaning of public life" (1958: 57, added emphasis).

The ability to acknowledge and listen to narratives told from different positions is crucial to our current position. There are two possible readings of those recent visions of the preconditions for politics: either as doomed in advance to search for something already lost or (the interpretation I prefer) as *returning* in a potentially reinvigorated way to the path of a politics possible through public practices of mutual respect (cf. Sennett, 2003).

Such practices of respect and mutuality must, of course, reach many sites and networks, from cultural production to formal politics to the world of work. What is necessary—Arendt's essential insight—is that those sites are connected, through a multitude of links, to a public space (and time) of shared significance and meaning. This is what I have, provisionally, called a "community without closure" (Couldry, 2000b: 140), a space that sustains the possibility of mutual openness to the uncertain accounts we are able to give of ourselves (and of each other).

The community without closure implied by the practice of cultural studies does not itself constitute politics, but it enacts one of its essential preconditions. Citizens' mutual respect for each other's inalienable capacity to be *agents* in the public world would be a space of *civility* in Balibar's special use of the term: a space not of politics, but where, acting together, we might work toward "creating, re-creating and conserving the set of conditions in which politics as a collective participation in public affairs is possible, or at least not absolutely impossible" (2004: 115). Needless to say, we do not yet have such a space of civility in the United States or United Kingdom, any more than we did when Williams imagined a "common culture" generated in time through the "full democratic process" (1958: 319). Can cultural studies contribute to the building of that space of civility? Maybe. Should it try? Surely yes.

But here, of course, cultural studies cannot act effectively if it acts alone. It must connect with other practices—not necessarily academic: what about trade unions or charities that share with cultural studies the aim of encouraging reflection and dialogue about the problematic preconditions of democratic politics? What about religious organizations concerned with encouraging greater mutual understanding across the important divides between Christianity and Islam or between religion and secularism?

In disciplinary terms, there is much for cultural studies to learn from political theory and political science that interrogates the proper process of politics (particularly deliberative democracy theory),[30] as well as from the whole range of work across the social sciences and the policy arena that examines contemporary inequality and power.

In all this, I have, inevitably, only begun to map what the contribution of cultural studies—a differently focused, differently connected cultural studies—might be both to the crisis of democratic politics and to the future practice of politics itself. If Derrida was right to compare the current condition of politics and political theory (remember, he wrote before the "war on terror") to a dark night swept ineffectively by searchlights (1997: 81), then academic work can at best provide what Jesus Martin-Barbero called, in another context, a "nocturnal map" (1993: 211) that "rather than synthesising knowledge," offers "a reorganisation of the analytic terrain" in a way that, we can hope, provides foundations for future action.

Yet, of course, even here the specific contribution of cultural studies as one discipline, taken by itself, can at best be modest. But it would hardly be trivial—not if, through its teaching and research practice, cultural studies helped enact a "public realm" (in Arendt's quaint but useful phrase) where it made sense for us, and as yet unknown to others, to exchange, critically and sceptically, the fragments left from earlier visions of politics and community. How else, we might ask, could something new and worthy of the term *politics* emerge?

Notes

1. This chapter began as a keynote address given at the "Community" conference at Trinity and All Saints College, University of Leeds, September 18–20, 2003; many thanks to the organizers, particularly Derek McKiernan and Michael O'Higgins, for giving me the original opportunity to develop these ideas. Thanks to Henry Giroux and Dave Hesmondhalgh for comments and criticisms of the original version.

2. For example, Beck (1997, 2000a), Held (1995), Sassen (2002).

3. See in particular my recent work on media rituals (Couldry, 2003a).

4. Cf. Corlett (1989) on "community without unity."

5. See Clifford (1990), Hannerz (1992), and for discussion Couldry (2000b: chapter 5).

6. On the latter, see Inglehart (1997), Klingemann and Fuchs (1995), Dalton (2002).

7. Cf. Ricoeur's attempt to displace Levinas's asymmetrical conception of morality within a broader, intersubjectively grounded ethics (Ricoeur 1992: 189–190, 337–340).

8. Cf. Couldry (2000b: 51) and Ferrara (1998: 14–15), discussing Mead (1940).

9. This is particularly clear in Honneth (1995: chapter 16).

10. Cf. James Tully's vision of multicultural constitutional politics (1995: 184). Note also that Ricoeur, like Derrida, draws on Aristotle's concept of friendship and reciprocity (1992: 181–194), but in a more precise and specific way.

11. For my view (that cultural studies is best conceived as a discipline or at least a distinct methodological site), see Couldry (2000b).

12. See Isin (2002), Giroux (2003a), Wacquant (2002).

13. See Adams (2005).

14. For the full text of this pernicious legislation, see http://www.opsi.gov.uk/acts/acts2005/20050015.htm.

15. See *Guardian,* August 8, 2005, 8.

16. Cf. Shabi (2005).

17. As I write, a new demonstration of this sort has been started in the United States where a dead soldier's mother, Cindy Sheehan, has camped outside George W. Bush's Texas ranch: see *Guardian*, August 10, 2005, 12.

18. Thanks to the Economic and Social Research Council for its financial support for this project (under Research Grant number RES143-25-0011).

19. Cf. Neuman et al. (1992); Gamson (1992).

20. I wish to emphasize that the gloss I offer here on the project and its potential significance is my own, and not necessarily that of my colleagues on the project.

21. Thanks to Tony Bennett for making this point in response to a related paper I gave at the 2002 Cultural Returns conference at St Hughs College, Oxford.

22. Note, however, that this is quite different from arguing, along with some Foucauldian positions, that *the political* is *merely* a construction, and nothing else is at stake in the term beyond the ceaseless constructions and discourses that play behind it. Much more helpful, if at first sight more "traditional," is the work of Paul

Ricoeur (discussed in detail later), which seeks to maintain connections between the political, moral, and ethical, thereby avoiding the ultimate incoherence of Foucault's Nietzschean attempt to stand "above" values (cf. Taylor, 1986).

23. For the distinction between *politics* and *the political*, see Wolin (1996).

24. For more details of this pilot, see Couldry and Langer (2005).

25. A fine exception is Croteau (1995).

26. For important but contrasting discussions of the relation between attention and knowledge, see Delli Carpini and Keater (1996); Zolo (1992).

27. Cf. Williams's moving vision of adult education as a mutual process of transformation between teacher and taught, underwritten by their equality as citizens (Williams, 1993).

28. There is some similarity here with John Keane's "postfoundationalist" notion of civil society (Keane, 1998: 53).

29. Cf. Dewey's account of the saturated U.S. "public" in the early twentieth century (1946: 137).

30. See, for example, Habermas (1989, 1996); Calhoun (1992); Benhabib (1996); Young (2000).

PART III
Ethics and Media

6
Beyond the Televised Endgame?
Reflections after 9/11

⟜

Any modern society whose institutions ... allow some voices to dominate the global media while others go unheard, establishes power that need answer to nobody, so entrenches vulnerabilities and erodes capabilities for some, if not for many, people. It secures rather than limits the likelihood of injury. Its institutions and practices will lead to avoidable injury that is *systematic* and will leave wide scope for individual action and inaction that injures *gratuitously*. It is a society that institutionalizes injustice.
—Onora O'Neill, 1996: 170 (original emphasis)

The public sphere is constituted in part by what can appear, and the regulation of the sphere of appearance is one way to establish what will count as reality, and what will not. It is also a way of establishing whose lives can be marked as lives, and whose deaths will count as deaths. Our capacity to feel and to apprehend hangs in the balance. But so, too, does the fate of the reality of certain lives and deaths as well as the ability to think critically and publicly about the effects of war.
—Judith Butler, 2004: xx–xxi

So far in this book we have asked what are the priorities for media research (chapters 2 and 3) and what (against the background of those priorities) can cultural studies (chapters 4 and 5) contribute to public discourse at a time when democracy isn't working and the world is embroiled in a dangerous and open-ended conflict between, as the U.S. government would have it, forces of "freedom" and forces of "evil." In those latter chapters, ethics emerged as a theme when we discussed cultural studies' position on the ethics of representation. In the closing section of the book, I want to recombine that focus on ethics with the agenda for media research discussed earlier by asking what might an ethics of *media* be like? In this chapter, I move toward this question by considering the risks, for all of us, of the global media system's being based on profound inequalities between world regions; shared risks change the conditions of action, and so have implications for ethics—how should we and media act in the face of those risks? I leave until chapter 7 the wider discussion of what is entailed by the term *media ethics*.

The focus of this chapter will be questions of power, and the consequences of major power imbalances that persist unchanged and apparently legitimated for long periods; in particular, power imbalances in access to the media infrastructure that produces the narratives through which the world's events are told from day to day. This may seem an abrupt shift from the last two chapters' discussions of the imaginability of democracy on the scale of national societies. On a *global* scale, it makes no sense for media and cultural studies to treat participatory democracy as an automatic value, since none of us yet knows what that would mean on a global scale. Yet that is not the end of the discussion. In Rousseau's original model (1973: 240), democracy was impossible except in territories small enough for citizens to meet face-to-face, but on a global scale, it is *human life itself* that may be unsustainable in the longer term unless some of the characteristics of democracy obtain—not necessarily a representative mechanism for popular participation in government (as yet, we have no world government, or the prospect of one), but at least *some* redistribution of symbolic resources such that large parts of the world are not absent from the process of constructing the major narratives of world events. For if the global media system is an institutionalized injustice (as the philosopher Onora O'Neill suggests in the initial quotation), then this injustice is likely to have consequences. How should we think about those consequences, and do they make necessary changes in the global media system itself?

The Conflictual Space of the Global Media System

I want to approach these difficult issues by reflecting on events that are both highly specific and controversial in their interpretation: the attacks on the World Trade Center on September 11, 2001 (for ease of reference, "September 11"). My approach to September 11 may diverge from familiar treatments. There were, of course, many dimensions of September 11 outside the expertise of a media specialist: issues of international relations, international security, the history of war. For media specialists, there were also many immediate and obvious priorities to research: the media coverage of the attacks and their aftermath, the storytelling devices and routines that developed as journalists sought to tell the story of an event that seemed to exceed all mere "stories," and the processes at work by which media institutions maintained, recovered, or reinforced their wider authority to represent the world in the context of those terrible events.[1]

Does this exhaust what media research can say about September 11? I suggest not, provided we move back a step, away from questions of media coverage, and toward the media landscape that was the background to these acts. We must bracket the idea that the September 11 attacks were completely detached from the normal causal flow of social life and politics, which underlay the standard claim shortly afterward that "nothing will ever be the same again." This is not a trivial point: as we know from Victor Turner's theory of liminal social processes (Turner, 1974), the claim of total transformation and disruption is a feature of many social crises, whose outcome, however, is not transformation, but rather the *restoring* of order, generally on the same terms as before (but newly legitimated).[2] To counter that lapse back into analytic business as usual, we must insist at the outset on reframing our discussion of September 11 in terms of the longer-term landscape in which it had meaning. I mean not so much the general landscape of world news stories (although what I say will impinge on that) as the landscape of global media production, the unequal landscape of "speaking positions," which I will argue was one context within which it is plausible that those terrible acts made sense to their perpetrators.

But already some will recoil. By talking about the *meaning* of the September 11 attacks, we move away from the emotive claims of many at the time that the perpetrators of these acts were "senseless animals." It is, indeed, more disturbing, as the political scientist Brendan O'Leary (2001) argued shortly afterward, to insist that these actions were not senseless, and not necessarily even motivated purely by transcendent values (such as religious values): what if, on the contrary, those acts were instrumentally rational (using Weber's distinction between "value" and "instrumental rationality"), that is, strategic acts addressing certain constraints and possibilities in a long-term, not temporary, field of action?

What can we say about this field of action? First, and obviously, that it had many dimensions: political scientists and religious scholars will variously locate it in the history of resistance to "Western" policy in the Middle East and debates within Islam about relations with "the West." What of media researchers? Surely, we must recognize behind both the symbolism and the extraordinary physical violence of September 11 a space that we have known well for a long time: the profoundly skewed global landscape of media and cultural production debated for more than two decades under the terms *media imperialism* and *cultural imperialism.*

To be clear, I am not calling for reinstatement of the theses of media imperialism and cultural imperialism[3]; that would be strange given the many powerful critiques they provoked.[4] But we need to hold on to the insight at the core of media imperialism and cultural imperialism debates: that at the level of the global media system, major inequalities of production input and cultural output are not only unjust but have long-term *political* consequences.

This remains a disruptive insight. It prevents us from taking the narratives presented as world news as given, from accepting "the myth of 'the world, now'" (to adapt Brunsdon and Morley, 1978: 87). It jolts us from ever thinking fondly that the space of *global* media can be the unconstrained "space of appearance" that Arendt (1958) imagined in ancient Greece and Rousseau imagined in the small town square (Rousseau, 1968: 126, quoted by Taylor, 1994: 48): if such a global fiction seems absurd in the abstract, let's take a close look at the media rhetoric in the immediate aftermath of the Live8 concerts on July 2, 2005, and we will see that its absurdity is no guarantee it won't occur!

We must go further. For the global media system (of news production, film production and distribution, and so on) is more than infrastructure: it generates a space for action, a space for real, not fictional, symbolic conflict in front of the world's cameras. The Indian political scientist Dipankar Sinha has called this space the "Global Information Order" (GIO); this space is very different from the World Information and Communication Order, challenges to which generated the media imperialism debate. The GIO, however much structured by inequalities, is a "shared space" (2004: 1), a space of action and representation. In this shared space, two fundamentalisms compete: the religious fundamentalism that lies behind the acts of the September 11 attackers and many others, and what Sinha calls "the other fundamentalism" associated particularly with the United States, that "define[s] and explains[s] the dynamism of the world in overwhelmingly Westcentric terms" (2004: 2). Although in some respects secular, this "other" fundamentalism is similar to religious fundamentalism because it, too, "would seek to establish a closed, homogeneous manipulable world order in which any alternative representation is devalued and discarded." These rival fundamentalisms share the symbolic resources of the GIO (even if the nature and scope of their resources are very different) and inhabit the space/time of "world events" that "order" sustains.

I want to argue that the inequalities of the GIO create risks that in the long run are unsustainable. Those risks must be reduced. This can only be done by a more even distribution of the world's media resources, and that is likely to be addressed effectively only in the very long term; in the mean-time, and in an environment of high risk, we need to consider the ethics of global media coverage—unless, that is, we are relaxed about being extras on the set of the world's televised endgame.

Refiguring What We Know

First, I need to give more substance to my claim that just as important as new empirical investigations into media and terrorism (at least right now) are reframing and reconfiguring what we already know about the global media landscape that provided the long-term context for September 11.

A Long-Known Injustice

My starting point is not the media imperialism and cultural imperialism debates so much (for it is only the essential insight from those debates on which we draw), but an area of media theory with which those debates are rarely if ever connected: I mean work on the "ritual mode of communica-tion" (Carey, 1989). James Carey in his well-known discussion argued that most communication analysis had seen media merely as the "transmission" of images and information across space, thereby ignoring another, and ar-guably more fundamental, dimension of media: media's continuous role in sustaining societies *in time*. It was the latter that Carey called the "ritual mode of communication." Since the media/cultural imperialism analyses came out of the political economy tradition, which has generally concentrated upon transmission,[5] it is hardly surprising that the importance of Carey's work for political economy, and for the GIO, has never been developed. But the connections are important.

The heart of Carey's discussion is a simple, but crucial, point: that media over time, and through countless complex influences, construct "reality," what passes for our "social reality." As he puts it: "Communication is a sym-bolic process whereby reality is produced, maintained, repaired and trans-formed" (Carey, 1989: 23); and elsewhere: "Reality is a scarce resource … the fundamental form of power is the power to define, allocate and display this resource" (Carey, 1989: 87).

Carey's work is rich but at times ambiguous in pursuing this insight's implications for an analysis of media power. Although sometimes he has foregrounded the conflictual dimension of the media's ritual mode and although, in the second passage quoted in the previous paragraph, he is explicit about the contests for the power to construct reality that underlie whatever consensus media sustain, at other times these dimensions of con-flict are less prominent in his work. This tendency to downplay conflict is a feature of the whole Durkheimian approach to media, which I have analyzed critically elsewhere (Couldry, 2003a). Once again, it is only the essential point of Carey's argument—not its details—that concern us here.

Carey's implied definition of *media power*—the power to construct and define social reality—is shared not only by other writers straightforwardly sympathetic to Durkheim's theories of the social bond (Dayan and Katz, 1992), but also by anthropologists and sociologists who have sought to adapt the Durkheimian framework to analyzing power and conflict. There are a number of authors I could discuss here, but to keep the discussion brief I will mention just one, Pierre Bourdieu. Bourdieu's definition of *symbolic power*—"the power of constructing reality" (1990: 166)—tracks Carey's terminology, but it places it more directly in a space of conflict and politics.

> The social function of ... symbolism ... is an authentic political function which cannot be reduced to the structuralists' function of communication. Symbols are the instruments *par excellence* of "social integration": as instruments of knowledge and communication ... they make it possible for there to be a *consensus* on the meaning of the social world, a consensus which contributes fundamentally to the reproduction of the social order. (Bourdieu, 1990: 166)

What are the implications of this? Most directly, that we need to take some distance from those moments such as the aftermath of September 11 when media appear to reflect and further define a consensual reality. Media studies has done this for decades, but more by analyzing how *specific* ideological conflicts are played out through the media than by noticing conflicts over the distribution of symbolic power itself. And it is this underlying dimension of conflict that is most relevant here, precisely because it was one crucial dimension of the September 11 attacks understood as symbolic actions.

This point is more easily absorbed in a national rather than a global context. On a national scale, there are, of course, ongoing conflicts about the priorities for media narratives and (although this is much less studied) over the conditions for entering that select group of people who produce media messages. This space of conflict can, for any one country, be encompassed into a general analysis of the media's involvement in national politics and struggles for hegemony. The analysis can be pursued in a self-contained way, at least in many countries, because of the assumption that the media in a particular country are, broadly speaking, *representative:* that more or less, and with many qualifications and limitations, the media are an institutional sector that for all sorts of reasons cannot simply bracket out social pressures from a wide range of sources without losing legitimacy in its national territory. This is fundamentally why, for example,

Dayan and Katz's (1992) well-known analysis of media events—as special moments when the complex and ultimately consensual power of television works—seems plausible.[6]

If, however, we consider questions of symbolic power and symbolic conflict on the global media stage, the analysis runs less easily. A whole mass of empirical work has given reasons why *in principle* we cannot assume that the global media screen is a more or less representative space. The key issues are as follows: first, the work on the structures of global media production and its increasing corporate concentration, which is likely to be intensified not dispersed, through the synergies of digitalized media production and circulation (Hermann and McChesney, 1997; Hesmondhalgh, 2002); second, the work specifically on how global news agendas are susceptible to influences from one small sector or network within the space of global politics (Hallin, 1994), rather than being reflective of that whole space; third, the important and empirically dense tradition of work on how the material infrastructure of news production (where are news agencies based, what resources do they have to produce news narratives, where do they tend to send their reporters and their cameras, and so on?) affects what can *be* an "event," what can *be* "news," and for whom and on what interpretative terms (Boyd-Barrett and Rantanen, 1998).

While denying neither the complexity of these debates nor the important caveat that Oliver Boyd-Barrett has always placed on their significance—the deliberate bracketing in the media imperialism thesis of how media flows influence actual audiences across the world (Boyd-Barrett, 1998)—there is, I would want to argue, a broad consensus that overall the structure of global media production and distribution is characterized by the most profound *inequality* in the distribution of symbolic resources. If so, when we think about the media's role of defining *reality* on a global scale, it is obvious that, whatever the apparent consensus and order, at least from perspectives based in the West, there is enormous scope for conflict, not only over particular news stories, but also over how the underlying inequality in symbolic resources limits the range of stories that enter the global news frame. Nancy Fraser (2000) has shown that issues of cultural recognition should not be separated from questions of the fair and even distribution of society's resources; lack of recognition results from an "institutional pattern of cultural value [that] constitutes some social actors as less than full members of society and prevents them from participating as peers" (2000: 113). Relevant here are symbolic resources including the ability to secure a media presence for oneself. This is precisely the type of injustice we see on a global scale, too. There is, in other words, an injustice embedded deep within the mechanisms for construing the world's reality (compare the quotation from Judith

Butler at the beginning of this chapter), an injustice that is integral, not incidental, to contemporary social analysis

The Potential for Conflict

If we see media as the site of reality construction, then underlying inequality in the media sphere is potentially the most fundamental dimension of social conflict. It is a conflict over the definition of all there is. As the Italian political theorist Alberto Melucci argued: "The true exploitation is not the deprivation of information ... the real domination is today the exclusion from the power of naming" (1996: 182).

By "naming," Melucci meant naming social reality, and he had both global and national media spaces in mind. From this perspective, the global media landscape is not a space of potential consensus, but a space of intense, if often repressed, conflict over symbolic power: a conflict over the right to name the world. For Melucci, there is constant struggle for influence over the "master codes" at work within dominant narratives. Because of the intensified concentration of information and image flows, the potential resonance of acts that directly contest those codes is broadened, too. The greater the replicating power of a code, the greater the resonance of acts that contest it, provided, of course, that they are played out in proximity to the distribution nodes of national or global media space (cf. Castells, 1997: chapter 6). The result is the likelihood over time of *an intensification*, not a reduction, of symbolic conflict across the global media landscape—not only for reasons of economic, political, or religious dispute, important though these may be, but for reasons directly linked to the scale of inequalities underlying that symbolic landscape.

In that context, the familiar debates about the complex local influences and negotiations of globally distributed media products (where media/cultural imperialism theses have been heavily criticized) are irrelevant. They are irrelevant since their reference point is an imagined (but wholly illusory) claim of cultural homogenization. As Ien Ang has pointed out, the real issue is quite different. *Global culture* (if we can use that term) is not a simple homogenization, but rather a universal shift in the "parameters and infrastructure which determine the conditions for local cultures" (1996: 153). It is precisely at this level of the *infrastructure* of the world's media and cultural production that the most powerful dimension of symbolic conflict arises. Even if there is no "perfectly coherent, unitary whole" of global culture (1996: 156), these structural inequalities shape the landscape within which all local strategies are pursued, including local strategies that result in "terrorist" acts such as September 11. The global media landscape with all its history of unequal struggles for the resources to name the world is a fully naturalized world with a particular form, whose focus is America. By "America," I mean the symbolic construction of America, which is, of course, inseparable from a real and vast concentration of the world's resources. From this perspective, whatever the subtleties of local appropriations of global products, it remains true that "the American system" is naturalized "as the insurmountable horizon of our time" (Mattelart, Delcourt, and Mattelart, 1984: 100–101). This was one thing September 11 did not change.

Although Jean Baudrillard (1983: 135–136) long ago argued that the Twin Towers had a detailed symbolic meaning—as a rhetorical doubling of a symbol of corporate power that thereby rendered power more opaque and unchallengeable—other symbols could have been chosen for attacks against corporate power. The Twin Towers were not precise symbols in themselves. Yet they had automatic resonance due to their visibility on the skyline of Manhattan—New York City is the world city that represents, more than any other, the concentration of various important production resources (financial, quasi-governmental agencies, and media). The Twin Towers were an automatic, even banal, *symbol* of that concentration of power (including symbolic power). To destroy that city's most prominent buildings was a direct act of *communication* (as Saskia Sassen insisted the day after the attacks: Sassen, 2001). Its resonance as an act of communication was already guaranteed by those buildings' availability as reference points, but it was massively amplified by the (envisaged, because inevitable) presence of live television. The communicative act of September 11 demanded a right to speak through the global media frame from a position of silence and invisibility, a temporary seizure of symbolic power by people whose position otherwise in the global media landscape was almost entirely marginal. The long unequal history of the global media landscape was one frame within which the attacks on New York's Twin Towers had meaning: if we ignore this, we fail to understand one vital dimension of those terrible acts. Yet, for all their violence, those acts did not destroy the American horizon, nor the historic inequalities that the naturalness of that horizon disguises.

Reviving the Debate on the Global Media Landscape

The immediate fears of a massive escalation of global conflict following September 11 did not materialize. Although terrible further acts have followed (Bali, Madrid, the attacks in London on July 7, 2005, just weeks before I write), none of them constituted an escalation, as opposed to a bloody continuation, of that conflict. But there is no reason to believe that this televised global endgame was closed with those early moves. The global media arena—surely the most powerful theatrical frame the world has ever known—remains open; the unequal symbolic landscape to which this frame is wired subsists unchanged. The global media landscape remains extremely unstable, not so much in its actual patterns of resource distribution (which remain, precisely, fixed), but in the *cultural consequences* of those inequalities. There is a parallel here with the cultural impacts of globalization more generally. Debates about globalization (including the "free trade" of cultural goods) often proceed as if the business flows underlying this unequal pattern had no cultural or political consequences; but, as Jeremy Rifkin (2001) pointed out, there is a serious question about whether, for all its prominent celebrants, what passes for the "globalization" of cultural flows is a process in equilibrium, or unsustainable in the long term.

Where does this leave us? First, there is no possible victory for anyone from this endgame of which September 11 was the most visible starting point, however long it lasts (here the symbolic endgame must be sharply distinguished from the American-led retaliatory "war on terror," which, of course, will have losers and winners). So what we need is a way out from the endgame, not a move up to its next stage. But I see no exit without a sustained effort to challenge the conditions that set the endgame in motion. Once again, let me emphasize that I can only consider the media aspects here, although they are, of course, connected with the others.

A starting point is to reject all practices that seek to sustain the West's globally massive concentration of symbolic power, particularly, in North America and Europe. Why? Not because that hegemony in itself is unsustainable—quite the contrary, as I've already suggested, it will go on being reproduced without the most enormous effort from many different directions—but because, by being sustained, it reproduces the conditions for the televised endgame, whose long-term unsustainability is surely obvious.

What types of practices are in question here? First of all, there are various cultural arguments that seek to legitimate an imbalance of power, for example, as the means toward winning the "clash of civilizations" in Samuel Huntington's (1997) well-known thesis.

Second, there is neglect. Media and cultural studies academics should be arguing for a continual suspicion of conceptual frameworks—wherever applied, whether in academic work, policy or legal circles, or media—that make it more difficult to grasp underlying global inequalities of symbolic power and their dangers. After September 11, British and other governments argued for global poverty reduction, saying that poverty is a cause of "terrorism"; whether material poverty is a significant causal factor is confused by the fact that the symbolic leader of those attacks, Osama bin-Laden, is a disaffected member of the wealthy Saudi elite. Leaving that point aside, we must remember that poverty applies to inequalities of *symbolic* resources, too. But in the case of symbolic resources there is a prior problem, which is the normal *invisibility* of those symbolic inequalities, precisely because they are inequalities in the ability to represent the world. As Nina Eliasoph has put it: "Not only are dominated people powerless, they lack the power to name their own powerlessness; the lack is itself a kind of powerlessness" (1998: 235). So we need to be more sensitive to the influence of inequalities in symbolic power on the apparently natural surface of "world events."

Third, we should be arguing for more caution in how global conflict is framed. In particular, we should argue for more care in using the word *terrorism* itself. Whatever connotations this word may be given, its basic meaning is clear: terrorism is organized violence for political ends that is distinguished, principally, by not being recognized as legitimate. As Weber famously argued, the modern state is based upon a mixture of consent and coercion, but one crucial component is the state's claim to the "monopoly of the legitimate use of physical force in the enforcement of its order" (Weber, 1947: 154). The distinction between state acts of violence and terrorism does not therefore depend on the nature or degree of violence involved, but on the competing claims over the legitimacy of violence; as Elliott, Murdock, and Schlesinger once put it: "State bullets inflict death and injury in just the same way as terrorist bullets" (1986: 275). It is impossible, however, as media scholars, to neglect the fact that what counts as legitimate violence, and therefore as terrorism, is a constant point of dispute and negotiation at various levels of media coverage, that reflect national state pressures (as Elliott, Murdock, and Schlesinger showed in their classic study of UK media's coverage of political violence in Northern Ireland). What counts on a global scale as terrorism is inseparable both from power relations between the world's states *and* the dominance of particular states' agendas over the highly centralized global system for generating news and news events. In other words, the term *terrorism* is hopelessly entangled with the very inequalities of the global media landscape that should, in part, be our concern. This is not, for one moment, to minimize the terror which the acts called terrorism cause: most violence, especially large-scale violence, creates terror. But, if we want to "think past terror" (in Susan Buck-Morss's phrase), the asymmetrical reference of the term *terrorism* will not help.

Fourth, as media academics, we need to develop a more general line of argument aimed at generating dialogue with media practitioners. The general argument would run as follows:

1. The inequalities in the global landscape of media production have real consequences in the shaping of the image of the world that policymakers, media and cultural commentators, and whole populations carry with them. These inequalities are an injustice that matters.

2. These inequalities also have consequences in terms of the range of alternative positions that can be heard and therefore in the degree to which the *complexity* of social and political space is reduced. This point applies on all scales, up to and including the global. Its importance does not depend on any transcendental reference point or truth standard, but, instead, on a materialist argument about the coarseness of our pictures of the world when the voices that contribute to that picture are restricted.

3. The coarseness with which the world's complexity is depicted has ethical consequences, too: for journalists who want to get that picture right, and for all of us when our own freedoms are affected by the ensuing risks. Inequalities in the distribution of symbolic resources have real consequences, as a potential cause of, and ground for, conflict.

4. As a result, the ways in which media practices respond to these inequalities and seek to adjust for them are not mere technical issues for journalist manuals but a central issue of social life. These are partly questions of media organization—what resources does a news organization need to represent effectively the global range of the sites affected by a major world event? They are also questions of value, requiring a change of priority over which sources are allowed to contribute to the images and information flows we receive as tokens of the world's events, and which are not. It would be misleading to deny that many journalists in the West are sensitive to these issues.[7] The question is how such debate can be sustained and deepened.

5. It follows that an analysis of the operational consequences of the inequalities of the global media landscape is not an incidental debate for media handbooks but an essential component of all current debates about the public world. Media ethics matter not only for discussions of citizenship and the future of representative democracy but also for the structures of world governance that mediate between all states, whether officially democratic or not. Nor is this analysis important only for negative reasons (for the avoidance of conflict and an escalation of a global endgame). Indeed, if our only reasons for encouraging this debate are defensive, we miss the key point that the inequalities of the global media landscape are directly an issue of global justice. They affect the conditions under which states, groups, and individuals can recognize themselves as effective agents.

6. The ethics of mediation are therefore a central thread in debates about the future of politics on a global scale. Researching those

ethics must encompass the major inequalities in the ability of different nations, groups, and individuals to be heard through the world's media system. Media practitioners and media academics should be working toward the long-term reduction of those inequalities or, if not, they should realize that failure to do so will have real consequences. In chapter 7, I explore the wider framework of ethical thinking about media in which these specific reflections can take their place.

Image and Word

That, in a sense, is the end of my argument in this chapter, but I want to look back on it and comment on a potential contradiction.

I began by arguing that the intensely regulated representational space of global media involves inequalities, and therefore major tensions, which were an essential part of the background to September 11. These inequalities are not just a matter for academic reflection but have real consequences. They are a dimension of wider inequality with long-term disruptive consequences on a global scale. These consequences are, of course, easier to see retrospectively after September 11, but they did not begin with September 11. Indeed, they were inherent to the global media landscape of the past twenty to thirty years. Once again, we must remember that this media landscape is only one dimension of a much more complex set of global inequalities, but as media researchers, we are entitled, and indeed obliged, to select from that wider space.

Then I argued for the importance of changing those conditions of inequality: opening up spaces for new voices to speak through the media, recognizing the cultural tensions that go with a profoundly unequal space of representation. All of which suggests that we need more media images. Isn't the likely result of this, however, not a reduction, but an *intensification* of the possibilities for symbolic conflict through increasingly crowded channels of communication? How can we assume that a more open global media system will contribute to a safer world?

Potentially there *is* a conflict between the need for media democratization—if we see it, simply, as bringing a proliferation of images—and the desire for less symbolic conflict and more political stability. We reach a fundamental crux here in the ethics of mediation. An important book in stimulating debate on media ethics has been Luc Boltanski's (1999) *Distant Suffering* on the media's enabling of long-distance compassion for others' suffering. Are the disadvantages of the limits and distortions built into the media process outweighed by the enhanced possibilities for emotional connection with distant others, without which politics in large, dispersed, and highly differentiated societies might become impossible? Boltanski's argument is primarily aimed at the implications of images of distant suffering for political theory and focuses on the ethical consequences of image consumption; my argument perhaps has raised a parallel dilemma concerning the ethical consequences of the infrastructure of image production. Arguments for the democratization of the global media system risk having as their unintended consequences an intensification of world conflict, as more, and more conflicted, voices enter the mediated arena of the GIO. Can this possibly be what we, any of us, want?

In an earlier published version of this chapter, I unhelpfully posed the resulting question in terms of a choice: between image and word. My aim was to provoke debate about the consequences of the media coverage we have.[8] I had been struck by the difference between, say, the UK *Guardian's* use of images of the destruction and *Le Monde's*. Much as I admired the *Guardian's* effort to provide a range of opinion on September 11 from the outset, I was worried by its foregrounding (along with the rest of the British newspapers) of images for their own sake, compared with *Le Monde's* more careful quarantining of images within a framework of print and comment. I was far from sure that "the rhetoric of the image" (Barthes, 1972) always helps us, since it may undermine the distance from which to reflect, to make different comparisons and connections, and grasp complexity, not simplicity.

It was a mistake on my part to pose the ethical question as a reductive choice: image *or* word. Clearly, we need both. The more pertinent question is which images and which words? Are there combinations of images and words that contribute negatively to the world we share? How can we begin to formulate an ethics of image and word, an ethics of media?

The answer is not "fewer images" as such: "The demand for a truer image, for more images, for images that convey the full horror and reality of the suffering has its place and importance. The erasure of that suffering through the prohibition of images and representations more generally circumscribes the sphere of appearance, what we can see and what we can know" (Butler, 2004: 146).

But that does not mean for one moment that we should automatically be satisfied with the mediated images we have. Images of "terrorists," which present them as "evil" do not contribute to better understanding of what "terrorism" is, and how "it" can be prevented. Nor, to take a slightly more subtle case, is there an automatic benefit from media circulation of the grainy surveillance camera images of the July 7 London bombers on the way to their lethal acts and self-inflicted death. On its front page on July 15, 2005, the *Independent* (incidentally, the leading opponent of the Iraq war in the British press) reproduced, against a blank white background, the surveillance image of one bomber, rucksack of explosives, we surmise, on his back, with the following headline: "7.20 am, 7 July 2005, Luton station. One man on a mission to kill."

To what understanding did the reproduction of this image contribute? To our understanding of the causes of the July 7 attacks or to our understanding of the suffering they caused? To an understanding of what "terrorists" look like, so we can look out for them in the future? Clearly, no in each case. But the image contributed to a mediated drama—it constituted a small fragment from the mediated arena of the global endgame. The image draws us in, as spectators, to that arena; as a *Guardian* editorial put it, uncritically, a few days later: "Among the unsung heroes of the tragedy of July 7 was the population of CCTV cameras in London and Luton, which played a key role in the identification of the bombers—*and have provided chilling images of mass murderers in action*" (*Guardian*, July 18, 2005, 19, added emphasis).

But using CCTV images as legal or police evidence is one thing; using their fragments for *spectacle* (the image was reproduced worldwide) is another. At a time when media institutions might be considering how they could contribute to greater mutual understanding, they (here at least) seem to be busy reframing images that, as they circulate, are likely to silence, not promote, dialogue: "*This* is what *they* look like." We cannot divorce the images and words media use from the "normative schemas of intelligibility" (Butler, 2004: 146) that work through them.

In chapter 4, we discussed the need for "open communication" that, at a time of global conflict, facilitates, on both sides of that conflict, the mutual acknowledgment and adjustment of political languages—the everyday languages that intersect with them: more, and more open, dialogue, not less. But it is not only people that can be in dialogue. When images "talk to each other," there is no process of mutual adjustment, reflection, or self-distancing, such as in dialogue between two persons. Images may reinforce each other, but they cannot question, or retract, the assumptions on which they are built.[9]

At a time of conflict, the ethics of the image-saturated arena of the GIO is not straightforward. At the very least, we must be ready to pose new questions. The leader of the Zapatistas, Subcomandante Marcos, was right in an article written well before the September 11 attacks to challenge the endless clash of images and counterimages of the GIO. In societies dominated by the "grand screen" of world news and world consumerism, contesting the narratives that *underlie* those images is far from straightforward: "In fragmented globalisation, societies are fundamentally media societies. The media are the big mirror which shows not what society is, but what it has to be. Overflowing with tautologies and visual proofs, the media society is short of reasonings and arguments. For such a society, to prove is to repeat" (Marcos, 2000).

What should be the response, he asks, of critical intellectuals to this situation?

> The test of progressive thinkers, those with sceptical hope, is hardly easy. They have understood the functioning of things and they must, such is their duty, reveal it, show it, denounce it, and communicate it. But, to do this, they must confront the neoliberal theology, and behind that the media, the banks, the great corporations, the army, the police forces.

> All this in the full light of a visual era (*en pleine ère visuelle*). That is their great disadvantage: to confront the powers of the image with, as their sole recourse, the word.

To suggest that the risky arena of the Global Information Order requires a more careful reflection on what type of images (and words) we need may for some be iconoclasm, a challenge to the core of media's role in contemporary societies. But this is to misunderstand: we need mediated images, for sure; it is a question of how to think about *which* images, and what are the consequences for our agency of the images we have.

We need, in a word, an ethics of media.

Notes

1. For an important analysis on this last point in relation to another terrible media event, although not quite of the same global significance, see Barbie Zelizer's excellent book on the media's strategies for constructing their narrative authority in relation to John F. Kennedy's assassination (Zelizer, 1993).

2. For a powerful attack on similar misreadings of a much less significant and disturbing media event, see Walter (1999) on the aftermath in September 1997 of the death of Princess Diana.

3. See, respectively, Boyd-Barrett (1977) and Schiller (1969).

4. For example, Sinclair, Jacka, and Cunningham (1996); Tomlinson (1991).

5. For an important recent exception, see Murdock (2000).

6. For a critique, see Couldry (2003a, chapter 4).

7. See, for example, Silk's (2003) analysis of U.S. press coverage of American Muslims in the immediate aftermath of September 11 to which early UK press coverage following the July 7 attacks has some parallels.

8. See Couldry (2001b) and the reply by Frosh (2001).

9. Not at least without a huge interpretative apparatus; but here we are discussing everyday media images, not gallery art.

7
Toward a Global Media Ethics

⊕

Many contemporary societies, and the whole world system, are profoundly mediated; yet their media institutions are profoundly unaccountable. Media narratives pervade private and public space; indeed, media are the main institutional sites where representations of social life get made, so much so that media freedom is widely regarded as a basic necessity for democracy. Yet neither the ethical responsibility nor the democratic accountability of media institutions is the subject of regular and open public debate, let alone effective practice.

If media are indispensable to democratic life, we might expect automatic agreement on the importance of citizens' (whom democracy is supposed to benefit) having an active say in how media institutions operate. Yet, while few are without an opinion on how media perform their responsibilities—as Onora O'Neill (2002: 90–91) puts it, "An erratically reliable or unassessable press ... for most citizens matters"—far fewer would expect their views to influence what media do. Fatalism about media rivals fatalism about politics, but without the safety valve of elections. This democratic deficit in relation to media has many causes, some good, some bad. Good reasons derive from media's tenacious defense of their independence from politicians and the state; that tenacity is essential if media are to contribute to democratic life. Bad reasons stem from something less healthy: journalists' (and others') use of "media independence" as a shibboleth to render illegitimate any outside moral or ethical scrutiny, in particular by citizens themselves.

Media institutions and their representatives, to be sure, have in most countries adopted explicit ethical codes of variable effectiveness, which are managed as the internal concerns of the media industries.[1] In addition, many individual journalists no doubt have ethics as their constant professional concern. But that is not the issue, any more than it would be sufficient, in a country where debate about politicians' ethics was discouraged, to argue that politicians themselves often agonize about the ethics of what they do! They may, but that is not the point. The ethics of media institutions, as institutions within the fabric of public life, constitutes a *public* question that is the proper concern of citizens as much as media professionals.

We cannot take democratic theory, let alone specific versions of democratic theory, as an agreed reference point for global debate in evaluating media. The reason is simple: like it or not, there is insufficient agreement about what democracy is or means. But, within the framework of *ethics,* we can suggest that if the purpose of media institutions is the circulation of information necessary for people to live well together in a territory (i.e., for their collective life to flourish), then whether media fulfill that purpose is a concern for everyone in that territory, *whether or not* it is a democracy. That argument applies on any scale, up to and including the territory of the world, and I will develop it here in the hope of laying some foundations for a global media ethics.[2]

By *ethics,* I mean neither a specific ethical code (as in some interpretations of the word) nor an agreed list of specific, and narrowly circumscribed, "virtues" (as in some versions of virtue ethics), but rather an open-ended process of reflecting on how we need to act so that we live well, both individually and collectively. I will explain later how ethics in this sense fits into the wider space of moral philosophy and morality. Much of the chapter is therefore taken up with what might seem like background to the principles of media ethics developed in its second half. But please be patient: when we lack, as currently, a framework for thinking about and formulating media ethics, we have to move slowly, step by step. Indeed, the first step is to recognize the absence of that framework from the public world, however saturated it is by media.

Media Ethics: The Unasked Question

Neither academic literature nor institutional practice offers adequate space for the discussion of media ethics. As a result, a deliberative practice that ought to be *central* to public life is at best a ghost, which we occasionally sense though it is unable to do much more than signal its potential presence. How has this occurred?

Academic Silence

There are, of course, many books that purport to be about media ethics. Media, like any profession, have "ethical" codes of practice; media training (with which some media research overlaps) involves disseminating, and reflecting upon, those codes. This is as true for journalists as for accountants. But none of us would look to accountancy training manuals for answers to (or even the formulation of) the wider questions about how accountancy fits into society's wider power relations. Why not? Because those manuals are *internal* to that practice and are designed, indirectly, to legitimate it within wider society, rather than reflect openly upon its ethical standing. Similarly, we are likely to be disappointed if we turn to professionally focused treatments of media ethics for a wider account of how journalistic codes might, let alone should, be assessed from wider ethical perspectives.

It is common for books on media ethics to fail to address what should be its two principal questions:

- What are the ethical standards by which media's *own* ethical standards should be judged?
- How do those broader ethical standards relate to more general principles for judging how citizens (whether media professionals or not) should behave in relation to media?

Discussion is often aimed at a specialist audience, internal to the media profession. Genuine media ethics lies largely outside the subject officially designated with that name.

The gap in the academic literature may take two distinct forms. First, discussions of media standards may fail to raise *any* wider questions about how the media's codes should be judged by citizens. Or second, and more interestingly, such issues are raised but detailed examination is quickly blocked off on the grounds that we already "know" the answers or that alternative answers are too implausible to be worth discussing—which illustrates, even if in reverse, what a media ethics might be about. So, for example, when Richard Keeble (2001) in a well-organized textbook on ethics for journalists turns to wider questions about journalists' role, he offers little more than a restatement of journalists' standard justification of themselves as guards against irresponsible political power. The point is not that this idea is wrong, but that *it is only the start of the discussion*. The way Keeble bolsters his position by quotations from other writers is striking. For example, he cites the communications theorist Denis McQuail: "It can be seen that social responsibility theory [in relation to media] has to try to reconcile three somewhat divergent principles: of individual freedom and choice, of media freedom, and of media's obligation to society" (Keeble, 2001: 131, quoting McQuail, 1987: 116–117).

Note how in the McQuail quotation individual freedom, media freedom, and media obligations are treated as if they were entirely separate principles (and so don't need to be formulated in terms of each other—not surprising therefore that they clash!); as a result, the question of their possible, perhaps necessary, *inter*relation is suppressed. Even more naturalized and resistant to unpacking, on the face of it, is this quote by Keeble from John O'Neill: "The free market, journalism and democracy form an interdependent trinity of institutions in an open society" (Keeble, 2001: 126, quoting O'Neill, 1992: 16). Not much scope here, it seems, to question how journalism should operate if it is to contribute to democracy, since the relationship is already taken for granted—this is certainly how Keeble uses the quotation. Strikingly, however, O'Neill's original point was the exact opposite of Keeble's: O'Neill was (plausibly) arguing that free markets in media prevent media's contributing adequately to democracy, so *blowing apart* the automatic trinity of market freedom, media freedom, and citizen freedom (1992: 16). This leads O'Neill to reexamine the wider grounding of journalistic values, rather than repeat "press freedom" like a mantra. Such scepticism, however, is absent from most textbook accounts of media ethics that maintain only a thin connection to the larger debates O'Neill raises.

The closing off of debate about the foundations of media ethics appears also in discussion of reforms to media practice. So Belsey and Chadwick in their edited collection *Ethical Issues in Journalism and the Media,* having pointed out that—by one plausible ethical standard: the avoidance of harm to others—bad reporting may do considerably *more* harm to individuals than physical aggression, then disable further questions by concluding that any external constraint on journalists to prevent such harm is inconceivable: "Nevertheless the idea that a journalist should be licensed to practise—with the license being removed for serious violations of a code of conduct [as in most other areas where a practice can do harm, author's clarification]—is surely too draconian and *antidemocratic* a solution to the problem of media malpractice" (Belsey and Chadwick, 1992: 9, added emphasis). Why? Belsey and Chadwick here close down debate by automatically equating unfettered media activity with democratic practice: precisely the assumption that a broader media ethics would open up.

This closure has a postmodern variant. It is true, no doubt, that journalistic ethics can no longer be considered only in terms of the standards operating for news and documentary: what, for example, of reality television and its relationship to entertainment values with a history outside documentary and current affairs programming (Turner, 2003; Lumby and Probyn, 2003)? In their programmatic introduction to a recent collection calling for a "new ethics" of media, Lumby and Probyn develop this point, but in a way that seems to avoid reexamining the substance of media ethics: "Any discussion of media ethics has to proceed from a detailed examination of how a given media text is organised, produced *and consumed*" (2003: 3, added emphasis). Of course, it is important to think about audiences at some level, whether in media ethics or anywhere else, but there is a danger that this new emphasis on "consumers" will become a celebration of consumerism, so obscuring the wider questions about the social ethics of media production that need urgently to be explored.

Dissatisfaction with the stifling of academic debate about media ethics has been voiced by a few dissenters. Particularly scathing is the Israeli legal philosopher Raphael Cohen-Almagor: "The liberal values that underlie any democratic society, those of not harming and respecting others, are kept outside the realm of journalism. As long as this is the case, the term 'media ethics' will remain a cynical combination" (Cohen-Almagor, 2001: 79).[3] Cohen-Almagor goes on to develop a framework based on the Kantian principle of autonomy with which to challenge ready-made assumptions about what events media should cover and how they should do so; in so doing, he opens up ethical questions about what media *do* in the exercise of their freedom. But such questioning is all too rare.

Institutional Neglect?

It is a measure of the failure of UK attempts to institutionalize effective self-regulation of the media that such academic neglect has not, at least in the United Kingdom, provoked major controversy. While the 1949 UK Press Commission recommended a body, originally to be called the "General Council of the Press" (compare the General Medical Council that regulates UK doctors), to "embody and promote a professional culture among journalists" (Curran and Seaton, 2003: 356), its implementation in various incarnations (most recently the Press Complaints Commission, 1991–) is still widely regarded as ineffective and desultory.[4] The verdict of two authoritative commentators is devastating: "The Press Council and PCC did not commission and publish substantial research, stage formative debates, honour leading journalists or restructure journalism education. Indeed, it never really embodied a professionalizing project. Unwanted by the press, it settled for being a customer complaints service, and discreet lobbyist for the industry" (Curran and Seaton, 2003: 357).

Little wonder then that this shadow institution failed to generate substantive debate about media ethics among the UK general public in the late twentieth century. The early years of the new century—marked in Britain by increasingly confrontational relations between media and a controversial, publicity-obsessed, New Labour regime under Tony Blair—saw the start of a shift, with the government being accused of too much "spin" and UK media being accused (Lloyd, 2004) of devoting too much time to inventing stories that encouraged suspicion of government culture. Fears about declining public engagement with politics were also a major factor, as a much-cited

BBC-commissioned research report emphasized (BBC, 2002). The philosopher Onora O'Neill's BBC-broadcast *Reith Lectures* (O'Neill, 2002) were also important in opening up the question of media accountability on a wider front. At the beginning of 2005, the first signs of a media debate on media's broader *ethical* standards emerged (Lambert, 2005; Williams, 2005), but they remain tentative.

Here the United Kingdom has in some respects lagged behind the United States. The United States too, in the aftermath of World War II, saw the publication of a major report, the 1949 Hutchins Commission's *Report on the Freedom of the Press*. Decades later, but still ahead of the United Kingdom, concerns at the complete vacuum of debate about the social and political consequences of media practice led to a reaction in the form of the vigorous "public journalism" movement in the 1990s (Glasser, 1999). This movement has had a high profile and stimulated much debate, fueled by prominent scandals over news standards (affecting over the past decade the *New York Times*, the *Los Angeles Times*, and other prestigious media institutions). The emphasis of the public journalism movement, however, is on how media should contribute to engagement in public affairs, not a broader debate on the ethics of what media do. There has been little broader debate on media ethics because of the predominance in the United States of a purely libertarian perspective that puts press *freedom* above all other considerations (Christians, 1989: 10). This quarantine around media ethics has for more than two centuries been buttressed by the protections on press freedom written into the First Amendment of the U.S. Constitution; whatever the abstract importance of that protection, the quarantine becomes damaging when interpreted as a protection for unfettered market activity rather than the support for democratic practice that the First Amendment originally intended (Sunstein, 1993; cf. Keane, 1991).

It would be foolish, of course, to suggest that the inadequacies of U.S. and UK institutions are necessarily typical of those of the rest of the world. Zambia has, for example, recently set up a Media Ethics Council[5]; media ethics is a live issue in many countries (South Africa, Latin America). But my general point is that the prevalent institutional models of media regulation do not encourage any link to broader questions of ethics, quite the contrary. It is significant that an authoritative international review of media ethics glosses the word *ethics* as "deontology," exactly the opposite of the sense in which I will use the term here.

Media Ethics and Christian Humanism

At this point, however, we must note a vital exception to the relative inattention to ethics in media research and media practice. This is the

communitarian-inspired U.S. tradition that in the view of one commentator (White, 2003) constituted a paradigm shift in thinking about communication ethics. White interestingly relates this shift to a concern with not
mainstream but nonmainstream or community media (an area I believe to
be of great importance)[6]; but here, in order to make the broader argument, I
want to focus on the possibility of an ethics of mainstream media. The fullest
attempt to develop an ethical perspective on mainstream "journalism ethics"
comes from the work of Clifford Christians and his U.S. colleagues.

   What is particularly impressive about Christians' work is its range, from
the details of how specific news stories are put together to a search for a
larger critical framework. Having trenchantly argued in a media ethics textbook that "journalism is [still] a profession *in search* of norms" (Christians,
Rotzoll, and Fackler, 1991: 417, added emphasis), Christians moved in 1993
toward arguing more ambitiously for "scholarship in media ethics ... of a
different kind" (Christians, Ferré, and Fackler, 1993: vi). Inevitably, this
involves choices as to the framework within which this wider media ethics
is based; Christians, Ferré, and Fackler opt for a communitarianism based
on the dialogic social ethic of the Christian theologian Reinhold Niebuhr.
Their aims are ambitious: namely, to stimulate "a fundamental reordering
of the press's mission, conventions and structures" (1993: 82) and "a fundamental restructuring of the organisational culture within which news is
constituted" (1993: 163).

   This approach is sensitive to the inequalities of power embedded in media practice, particularly media institutions' own power (Christians, 1989:
11), and critical of the hegemony of liberalism with its atomistic view of the
individual citizen (1993: 10). Instead, they search for "a dialogic communication theory in the phenomena of human encounter" (1993: 14). Nor do
they avoid questions about media's role in wider politics; on the contrary,
they insist that "civic transformation [should be] the press's occupational
norm" (1993: 14).

   Here, for the first time, was a large-scale attempt to develop a media
ethics in the broader sense: a framework within which journalistic "ethics"
might be *assessed* for its ethical adequacy. It is this move on which I want to
build in this chapter, even though the framework within which I will work
is quite different. The work of Clifford Christians and his colleagues, for
all its boldness and originality, is, I suggest, too steeped in the values of a
religiously, culturally, and geographically *particular* "social ethics" to be
persuasive on a global scale. Certainly, these authors raise the question of
normative pluralism and global dialogue (1993: chapter 6). When pushed,
however, to define what their own values (of "justice, compassion, reciprocity and stewardship": 1993: 176) are based on, they resort to a notion of
individual self-transformation, deriving from St Augustine[7]; Robert White

(2003), in his version of communitarian media ethics, draws on the notion of dialogue as a central human value. While both individual self-transformation and dialogue are important values, they fall short of offering a *general* framework for formulating values in relation to media; dialogue, for example, only makes sense within a wider evaluation of human community that requires specific justification and that runs the risk of being either exclusive or vacuous.

What we need, I suspect, to advance a global debate on media ethics is something different: an open framework for formulating *questions* on media ethics that is shorn so far as possible of the details of specific worldviews, yet, as Christians and his colleagues suggest, based in some stance on questions of value—some sense of how "the good" for human beings might, consensually, be understood. In the rest of this chapter, I will draw on the tradition of ethics, particularly aspects of the recent neo-Aristotelian tradition of virtue ethics, in order to move toward such a framework.

A Note on Public Sphere Theory

Before moving on, I must first acknowledge another area where media research has evaluated consequences of media at least in relation to politics. For there has been extensive debate for two decades or so in North American and northern European media research about the implications for democracy of media organization. This debate reached its greatest intensity in the United States and the United Kingdom following the English publication of Jurgen Habermas's book *The Structural Transformation of the Public Sphere* (1989). Habermas's explicitly normative model of how democracy should work, and how media should contribute to those workings, drew on a much-disputed historical sociology as well as a particular perspective on democratic theory (Calhoun, 1992). In spite of its particularity, Habermas's model generated a context in which, for example, the UK tradition of critical political economy analysis of media could propose its own normative models (Curran, 1996, 2000), similarly in Scandinavia, where Habermas's work was absorbed much earlier in its original German version (Dahlgren, 1995). Those countermodels aimed to think differently, and beyond the confines of liberal models, about how media should be organized if they were genuinely to contribute to the conditions for democratic politics. In the United States, similarly, the long tradition of critique of the media industries' economics (e.g., Hermann and McChesney, 1997) intersected not only with Habermas's model (although to a lesser degree than in the United Kingdom) but also with centuries' old legal and philosophical debates about media's legitimate role under the First Amendment of the U.S. Constitution. Recently C. Edwin Baker (2002) provided an extremely helpful overview of the U.S. debates and how they intersect specifically with public sphere debates in Europe.

I don't want, for one moment, to minimize the importance of such work. It is a vital part of the edifice of critical media and cultural research, to which this book aims, in its own way, to contribute. Nevertheless, debates on how the large-scale *organization* of media contributes to democracy are quite distinct from media ethics.[8] The former deal with the problems of scale and balance to which media—as industries for the production of social representations—give rise *regardless* of our view of the ethics of what journalists do. There are connections, of course, since the values underpinning the former—for example, democratic participation—provide part of the context for the values involved in the latter. The two debates, however, have a different status and purpose. Media ethics inquires after the possibility of consensus over how media should operate and how we should interact with media—whatever our views about large-scale principles of media organization. Media ethics, like ethics generally, would be impossible if every ethical question had to be routed first through a consideration of how the space of democratic politics should be organized. Correspondingly, it is not surprising that even Habermas's most developed version of his public sphere theory (Habermas, 1996) contains no reflections on the *ethics* of media practice.

This separation of public sphere theory and media ethics is in fact helpful: it allows us to see better the independent contribution media ethics can make to enhance dialogue between worldviews opposed not just on the details of democratic theory but even on the principle of democracy itself. For a global media ethics, this independence from political theory is vital.

What Is Media Ethics?

To get a sense of what we might mean by media ethics, let's begin in general terms. Ethics is concerned, first, with how we should act, and second, with how, consensually, to build a framework for thinking about how we should act. Ethics aims at a reasoned and inclusive debate about value, rather than a search for moral absolutes or systematic rational frameworks of moral justification—or at least that is the approach to ethics from Aristotle onward, on which I want to draw.

Ethics in this sense addresses the issue of how we should live. On the face of it, it might seem paradoxical to draw on philosophical ideas first formulated in ancient Greece to address the late modern phenomenon of a media-saturated society. Certainly, the pervasive mediation of action—our actions, and those of others, whether powerful or powerless—raises new questions about how, responsibly and ethically, we can and should act in the world. But why expect to find a suitable ethical framework available "off the peg" like a suit of clothes? Better to build our framework from elements found across the whole history of ethical thought. As it happens, aspects of the Aristotelian approach to ethics (so-called virtue ethics) have in the past two or three decades been revived more generally across philosophy and have been found useful precisely because of the openness of the questions that they generate. The fact that Aristotelian ethics have their source separate from today's predominant religious frameworks—including Judaism, Christianity, and Islam—is itself useful for a world where dialogue between major religions, and standpoints on religion (including secularism), is essential for a viable global politics, yet difficult to achieve.

Another advantage of the Aristotelian ethical tradition (whether in its original fourth-century B.C. or recent, neo-Aristotelian transformations) lies in the simplicity of the questions it asks. Two questions are fundamental:[9]

1. How should I live?
2. Depending on (1), how should each of us conduct our life so that it is a life any of us could value?

The first question is the question reputedly posed by Socrates, and its usefulness derives from its openness. As Bernard Williams argues, it is this openness (contrasted with specific questions about what it is right to do in this or that context) that makes it a suitable starting point for the study of ethics:

> [Socrates' question] is anybody's question ... when the question is put before me in the Socratic way, to invite reflection, it is going to be part of the reflection, because it is part of the knowledge constituting it, that *the question can be put to anybody* ... it very naturally moves ... to the question "how should anybody live?" That seems to ask for the reasons *we all* share for living in one way rather than another. It seems to ask for the conditions of the good life—the right life, perhaps, for human beings as such. (Williams, 1985: 20, adjusted emphasis)

The second question develops the first question into a model of virtue for the individual human life in general, which, since it can be addressed to and of anyone, is also, implicitly, a model for how we should live *together* (we have no choice but to attempt to live together). Note that no assumption is made here about the "community" (if any) to which questioner and respondent belong: they could be *any* two individuals. Indeed, these questions remain useful even if we no longer hold to Aristotle's assumptions about human nature and its necessary ends; the basic form of the Aristotelian question can survive the transition to a contemporary world where there are more complex disagreements about value than could be imagined in ancient Greece (Williams, 1985: 48, 53).

Media ethics then adjusts the second question to ask a specific media-related question:

3. How should any of us (whether media professionals or not) act ethically in relation to media?

Or, more precisely:

3A. How should we act in relation to media and the use of media resources, both individually and together, so as to conduct our lives in a way that we can value?

This generates a further question, if we lack a framework within which agreed standards of media ethics can be assessed:

4. In the absence of agreed standards for ethical conduct in relation to media, how can we build a framework within which such standards might be formulated?

I realize that even to ask such questions betrays, in the eyes of some, a naïve faith in discredited notions, such as a universal notion of "truth"! The debate over universalism (and the status of notions such as "truth" and "knowledge") that has weighed so heavily in media and cultural research over the past two decades is, however, more apparent than real (in this sense, poststructuralism has been a detour from which we are only just emerging); indeed, some leading poststructuralist doubters of universalism themselves returned in later years to the importance of truth, at least as a regulative ideal (see Norris, 1993, on Derrida; and, specifically in relation to media, Derrida and Stiegler, 2001).

Let's be under no illusion. Even if we can successfully disarm antiuniversalist attacks on the notion of truth (Williams, 2002), constructing a satisfactory media ethics is hardly simple; it involves, necessarily, a huge *collective* journey across the contemporary theoretical, social, political, and cultural landscape. Here we can, at most, take some initial steps in this direction.

Later in the chapter, I propose five principles as a consensual starting point within which detailed questions of media ethics can be discussed. As principles, they are quite simple and general. Once we agree, as a preliminary, that media institutions are not exempt from ethical accountability (why should they be, even if this is the position de facto at present?), we should be able to agree that media institutions—indeed, all of us when we become involved in the media process—ought to act in accordance with the two truth-related virtues of accuracy and sincerity (principle 1 under

"Media's Reflexive Virtues" in the section "Some Modest Proposals for a Media Ethics"). Less automatic, but flowing directly from the media's own claims to be necessary for democracy, is the idea (principle 2) that the aim of virtuous media practice should be to contribute not to profits, but to the successful individual and collective lives of the inhabitants of territories in which they operate; this in turn requires (principle 3) open public reflection by media institutions on how well they comply with the first two principles. If the first three principles are accepted (as the basis of a media ethics), then more difficult questions arise about the consequences for media institutions—or, indeed, any of us involved in the media process—of falling short of virtuous behavior. I propose two further contrasting principles (4 and 5 under "Defending Press Freedom, Limiting Press License" in the same section) that insist on media's responsibility for any harm they do to private individuals, but strengthen the protections around media's freedom to challenge powerful institutions without unnecessary legal challenge.

More details on these principles later. But first, since our main aim is to build from the foundations upward a framework for debate about media ethics, we must spend some more time on preliminary questions: (1) What exactly is at stake in the word *ethics*? (2) What might the notions of virtue, and specifically "communicative virtue," contribute to media ethics?

Why Media *Ethics*?

Ethics, Not Deontology

The distinction between approaches to morality based on notions of the good (ethics, virtue)[10] and those based on a notion of the "right" (duty, deontology) has been a fundamental fault line in contemporary moral philosophy.[11] It is with some trepidation that I say anything about it, but this cannot be avoided, since I must explain why I prefer the first approach over the second.

The fault line can be summed up historically in the difference between Aristotle's question "What is the good life for human beings?"[12] and Kant's question "What actions are the duty of any rational being?" Aristotle's approach, however broad its ambitions might seem to be (relating as they do to human life in general), remains specific—specific, that is, to the form of life called "human"—whereas Kant's approach is as general as possible, addressing *any* rational being. This is a crucial difference because Kant's "transcendental idealism" aims to stand above the things that human beings might from time to time *decide upon* as good and. indeed, to stand above the details of any particular form of life; this abstraction may, as we will see, be unhelpful in considering the historically specific challenges that media pose in today's conflicted world.

Why exactly do I use the word *ethics* to characterize my approach to evaluating media? Because it is this word, not *morality*—that is usually associated with the historical tradition from Aristotle onward concerned with what is the good for man, rather than with man's obligation (Williams, 1985: 1); in fact, the difference in the terms is pure convention, since both *ethics* and *morality* have their origins in classical terms for custom, one Greek and the other Latin, but let's leave that point to one side. The *ethics* tradition is sometimes referred to as *teleological* because Aristotle's ethics was based on the search for principles that best enacted the "end" (in Greek, *telos*) of human life; by contrast, the tradition flowing from Kant is often called *deontological* because of its emphasis on obligation and duty rather than good (once again, *deontological* comes from a Greek word, this time for obligation).

While there are complications here (it is possible to follow in the tradition of *ethics* without believing in Aristotle's teleology, and some philosophers now argue that it is the compatibilities between the two traditions that are important),[13] the basic distinction between *ethics* and *morality*, *teleology* and *deontology*, is important in thinking about what media we want and need. It represents the difference between, on the one hand, searching for some open-ended and quite general principles (not a comprehensive system) about how media should act, upon which at a particular place and time people might come to agree; and, on the other hand, searching for a comprehensive and systematic specification of moral rules with which any rational being could be expected to agree in relation to media. Note that pursuing the first approach in preference to the second acknowledges no more than a historical link to Aristotle's particular views on ethics, whose details and subsequent historical uses are hardly uncontroversial.[14] But there is no problem here since we have plenty of scope for flexibility in interpreting the tradition of *ethics* (not morality) in relation to media.

The difference, however, between the traditions of *ethics* and *morality* has contemporary philosophical significance because one of the most influential positions in late twentieth-century moral and political philosophy (John Rawls's work on justice and liberalism) chose the second, not the first, approach. For Rawls, the primary question is always that of justice and this question, from the outset, is sharply distinct from whatever individual views you or I might have on the good: "Just as each person must decide by rational reflection what constitutes his good, that is, the system of ends it is rational for him to pursue, so a group of persons must decide once and for all what is to count among them as just and unjust" (Rawls, 1972: 11–12). The question of the good (i.e., the end or ends toward which each of us should live our life) is for Rawls a question for individuals alone, quite separate from a theory of justice, and too uncertain to be helpful in this context. Not that the idea of good or virtue disappears from Rawls's theory; indeed, as Paul Ricoeur has argued, it remains a necessary assumption within it, even if suppressed in importance—consider the first sentence of *A Theory of Justice*: "Justice is the first virtue of social institutions, as truth is of systems of thought" (1972: 1, discussed in Ricoeur, 1992: 197). Indeed, in Rawls's later model of "political liberalism" (1996), the importance of political virtues (which sustain Rawls's developed account of justice) is asserted with great force.[15] All the more reason, perhaps, to start out from a consideration of what is virtue—the good for us, as humans—given the intractability of general questions of justice and fairness.

There are other, more positive, reasons for choosing ethics, not deontology. Bernard Williams offers an impassioned defense of ethics for its flexibility, open-endedness, and nontotalizing approach:

> [Morality's] insistence on abstracting the moral consciousness from other kinds of emotional reaction or social influence conceals not only the means by which it deals with deviant members of its community, but also the virtues of those means. It is not surprising that it should conceal them, since the virtues can be seen as such only from outside the system, from a point of view that can assign value to it, whereas the morality system is closed in on itself. (Williams, 1985: 195)

Williams's target here is Kant's dream of securing purely rational foundations to morality and Rawls's original attempt (modified later) to derive justice as a system of principles acceptable to all rational beings. But Williams's argument against deontology is relevant also to recent arguments that draw on Emanuel Levinas's attempt to rethink moral obligation as an absolute that cuts across any contextualized sense of value or rationality (Bauman, 1992; applied to media by Silverstone, 2003). So Williams helps us clarify what might be distinctive about the approach to media ethics developed in this chapter.

This does not require us, in pursuing a media ethics, to ignore the deontological tradition entirely. Indeed, we will not. Some eclecticism is reflected in Williams's own later writings (2002), where he draws on Kant's account of freedom in order to explicate the virtues of truthfulness. Similarly, within a broadly Kantian perspective, Onora O'Neill (1996: 8) has argued that it is unhelpful (and, within the longer history of philosophy, eccentric) to separate questions of obligation from questions of virtue. O'Neill also drops Rawls's requirement for a framework that compels acceptance on purely rational grounds (thus requiring us to make implausible assumptions about people's level of rationality); instead, she suggests a "more guarded constructivism" (1996: 48) that merely searches for principles that "all in the relevant domain *can* follow [i.e., whether they are completely rational or not]" (1996: 50, added emphasis). This connects with Philippa Foot's arguments, from within a firmly Aristotelian viewpoint, for removing the artificial division between questions of justice and questions of good (2000: 68). We should also note Paul Ricoeur's important attempt to reconcile deontological and teleological frameworks, by arguing that their respective sets of questions (what is good for human beings and what is just or right) are necessarily in dialogue with each other (Ricoeur, 1992: 170–171 and chapter 8); although for Ricoeur the question of the good remains prior to questions of justice, since it is the orienting framework within which the practice of justice itself has value. It is Ricoeur's position that matches most neatly my attempt here to develop a media ethics, while bracketing out, initially at least, questions of justice in the media sphere and drawing on an eclectic spirit of deontology.[16]

Addressing the Absence of Moral Consensus

At stake, however, in the choice between deontology and ethics is more than academic flexibility. There is a question about how we can address the obvious lack of consensus on substantive morality within (let alone beyond) large complex societies such as the United States and the United Kingdom.

There are, however, two quite different ways of addressing this distinctively modern problem. Bernard Williams (and here he differs from many virtue ethicists) argued that it is absurd to believe there is now consensus around the "ends" of the human species of the sort believed in by Aristotle (1985: 52); in later work Williams offers a "genealogy" of truth-related virtues such as accuracy and sincerity that deliberately avoids claiming to have discovered, or confirmed, principles binding for humans at all times and all places (2002: 34). Williams's cautious historicist reworking of the Aristotelian question (how should we live?) acknowledges the *lack* of consensus over moral values in a world of huge historical and cultural differences (2002: 122), while searching for other ways to achieve consensus over underlying principles, such as truthfulness. Interestingly, Rawls, within the deontological tradition, also addresses the intractable differences over the good that divide humanity. In *Theory of Justice,* as we have seen, he does this by excluding entirely the question of how individuals choose the "good" for themselves, while still believing he can assume we all share "an intuitive conviction of the primacy of justice" (1972: 4). However, by the time of *Political Liberalism,* he acknowledges that even this cannot be assumed (1996: xviii). The central problem of "political liberalism" for Rawls then becomes how is a "just society of free and equal citizens" possible, given the lack of consensus on fundamental issues even among those who are reasonable (1996: xx).

Yet these two strategies for dealing with the absence of moral consensus are strikingly different. Whereas Williams seeks to overcome it by arguments that reveal alternative areas of agreement (e.g., over the virtues of truthfulness), Rawls's strategy is to exclude the good (the area of apparent disagreement) entirely from his argument and look instead for principles of fairness that any rational person might agree upon, whatever she thinks about the good. The problem, however, is that even Rawls's principles of fairness, and the model of rational individual choice through which they are argued, are themselves contentious, and based in quite particular values, as Perry Anderson has shown in a recent discussion of Rawls's later work (2005).

Remember that our requirement of an ethical framework is that it helps us assess media's contribution to a world riven by major *differences* of value, and it becomes clear why it may be better to adopt something closer[17] to the spirit of Aristotle's "naturalism" as our starting point, rather than Kant's transcendental idealism (Lovibond, 2002: 25).[18]

A Flexible Naturalism

Clarifying what we might mean by such a flexible naturalism in media ethics should clarify also the degree to which we can move away from the details of Aristotle's own position on ethics, while remaining broadly within the tradition of ethics, not deontology. This is important in answering those for whom the mere mention of Aristotle seems unhelpful in contemporary contexts!

A naturalist approach allows for a continuous rediscovery of what constitutes human "nature." By contrast, what is often presented as Aristotle's original ethical position (which now has few followers) insists that human nature is fixed for all time; Martha Nussbaum (1993), however, argues that this is to misread the flexibility built into Aristotle's own account. However that may be, Nussbaum eloquently expresses the advantages of a flexibly naturalistic account of human virtues that "unlike some systems of moral rules remain[s] always open to revision in the light of new circumstances and new evidence . . . [so it] contains the flexibility to local conditions that the relativist would desire—but ... without sacrificing objectivity" (1993: 260). Other philosophers have extended the flexibility inherent in Aristotle's position (without necessarily claiming to follow Aristotle himself). Human nature, it can be argued, includes precisely the ability to live not only by certain fixed principles distinctive of the species (what we might call our "first nature") but also within a *historically adjustable* set of principles John MacDowell has called "second nature" (Lovibond, 2002: 25, discussing MacDowell, 1994: 84). A "naturalistic" approach to ethics involves grasping that "it is natural to us [human beings] to participate in a history that is *more than merely* natural" (Lovibond, 2002: 63, added emphasis).[19] The key to this second nature is open dialogue about our history as well as our ("fixed" but reflexively revisable) nature, and this leads to an account of communicative virtues (Lovibond: 2002: 78) on which there is more in the next section.[20]

It is in this spirit that I want to explore the possibilities for a framework of media ethics, since media foreground two specific aspects of our second nature: first, and most obviously, the historical emergence of institutions for representing whole societies—indeed, the world—that we call media; and second, the multiple incompatibilities of worldview that are inherent in global cultural interaction (cf. Buck-Morss, 2003: 93). For a media ethics—indeed, any ethics—confronts a global space, not a neat world segment (such as the nation-state where we might still imagine consensus on more specific values). Just as two decades ago, Hans Jonas pointed out that modern ethics faced a new type of problem from classical ethics, namely, the long-term effects of human technology on nature (Jonas, 1984: 1), so too we cannot now exclude from ethics the consequences media messages have for social and cultural life. Both problems—technology/nature and media—require not just a local or national but a global scale of analysis. Thinking on the global scale in relation to media audiences means acknowledging those who may share, on the face of it, *few* ethical principles with the producers of those messages.

This means that media ethics must address media's contribution (positive or negative) to the possibilities of living well together *without* reference to underlying religious, moral, and scientific principles (since it is precisely those on which we cannot assume consensus). The "imperative of responsibility" (in Jonas's phrase) for media ethics is based on the need to reflect about our most fundamental *dis*agreements (and their implications for how media should operate), not on the hope of some phantom global consensus or an all-encompassing rational resolution.

Only the most open question can serve as the starting point for this search: hence my preference for ethics' underlying question—how can we live together well?—over any other.[21]

Communicative Virtues?

In seeking detailed philosophical grounding for a specifically *media*-related ethics, Philippa Foot's bold defense of an account of moral judgment—based not in abstract rationality but in "essential features of specifically human life" (2000: 14)—is a useful starting point, since Foot was one of the first to turn to Aristotelian virtue ethics in Anglo-American philosophy. Her fundamental principle is what Elizabeth Anscombe (1997) called "Aristo-telian necessity," that is, "where something is necessary because and in so far as good [or the possibility of good] hangs on it" (Foot, 2000: 15). What is interesting for us here is that, although Foot does not explicitly alter the original Aristotelian view that the good for humans is based on what is necessary for humans *as a species,* her notion of "species good" is consider-ably more flexible than might first appear. At certain points (2000: 15) she offers, as an alternative, the notion of "life form" (borrowed from Michael Thompson, 1995), a formulation that invites us to consider how human life forms might under historical circumstances change (2000: 29).

There is, then, an inherent ambiguity in strict versions of Aristotelian virtue ethics such as Foot's that argue from the supposed "natural habitat" for the human species (Foot, 2000: 34, 36). What is the natural habitat (or, perhaps better, the "accepted ethical starting conditions") for the human species at the start of the twenty-first century? The necessities for human "preservation" in the early twenty-first century (when we have no choice but to live in a mediated, interconnecting global space) may be rather dif-ferent from the twelfth century when, as Onora O'Neill points out, it was quite sufficient to think about ethics or morality, whether in ancient China or medieval Europe, without attention to the consequences of decisions in one region on the survival of the other (O'Neill, 2000: 186–187). However, this does not undermine the usefulness of the fundamental question from which Aristotelian positions start: "One tries to determine what, given the circumstances, it would be good or bad in itself to do or to aim at. These questions are referred to larger ones: what kind of life it would be best to lead and what kind of person it would be best to be. The sense of 'good' and 'best' presupposed in this noncalculative form of practical thought is very general" (Quinn, 1995: 186). There is space, then, for other (not strictly Aristotelian) answers to the questions Aristotle first raised, especially if we acknowledge that humanity is a species that has progressively transformed its living conditions in crucial respects.

This is exactly what Sabina Lovibond's account of virtue, and specifically communicative virtues, provides. We have already touched on the idea of an open, historically dynamic naturalism on which Lovibond's argument is based: the idea that human nature is distinctive because of its propensity to develop a second nature that is open to historical transformation (2002: 63), including reflections on the historical transformations represented by media. This does not, however, mean there are no constants in ethics (cf. Nussbaum, 1993): at every stage of their history humans have had an interest in "gathering correct information about their environment" (Lovibond, 2002: 77), which requires them to be able to rely on what oth-ers tell them about that environment. From here Lovibond develops the useful notion of *communicative virtue:* "If information about deliberatively relevant circumstances is (so far as it goes) a natural good, the lack of such information is equally a natural evil and the benefit or harm we can incur from these sources brings communicative behaviour within the scope of ethics" (2002: 78).

Communicative virtue, Lovibond argues, necessarily entails being as serious in considering the consequences of one's falsehood for distant others as for those close to us (for there is no ethical reason distinguishing one audience from another): "Only what is epistemically good enough for anyone is good enough for one's present audience" (2002: 84). Lovibond acknowledges that this goes beyond Aristotle's rather narrow discussion of truthfulness and deception among friends,[22] but how else, we might add, to address in ethics the potentially global nature of today's information environment? Should an expert reporting on the Earth's atmosphere to a U.S. scientific conference consider the consequences of his untruthfulness only on his immediate audience? Of course, a wider global audience must be considered, because they may very soon receive the news of what she says, whether from a press release issued by the conference organizers, from a conference Web site, or from journalistic sources. It is the advantage of Lovibond's account of the *historicity* of virtue (2002: 133) (and, incidentally, Williams's and MacIntyre's too) that it can easily adapt to this aspect of the contemporary mediated environment.

The Virtues of Truthfulness

We need now to turn to the specific connection between communicative virtues and truth.

Here by far the most detailed treatment is provided by Bernard Williams in his book *Truth and Truthfulness* (2002).[23] It is impossible to summarize the subtleties of Williams's account of the two basic "virtues of truth" (2002: 44), "accuracy" and "authenticity." But a key feature is his attempt to defend the persistent, *nonnegotiable,* importance of these virtues for human social life, while at the same time rejecting any assumption that particular embodiments and articulations of those virtues (and the particular institutionally backed sanctions that apply when we fall short of them) have an absolute status for all historical periods. Williams is very far from arguing for virtues that are fixed, ahistorical reference points. Yet again there is some stability. It has never, Williams argues, been enough for people to *pretend* to care about telling the truth, since if that were all they did, then we would never have a stable basis for relying on them to tell the truth: "The reason why useful consequences have flowed [for humanity] from people's insistence that their beliefs should be true is surely, a lot of the time, that their insistence did not look just to those consequences but rather toward the truth" (Williams, 2002: 59). It is only therefore if truth telling is regarded as a virtue (as a *disposition* upon which humans can rely) that it contributes to the good collective life.[24]

This is where Williams's rejection of deontology, and insistence on ethics, comes into its own. For Williams rejects the deontological position (from Kant right back to Plato) that telling lies is "just wrong" and an affront to our status as rational beings (2002: 106). Instead, he accounts for the virtue of sincerity in terms of the link between truthfulness and trust; more precisely, (1) trust is a necessary precondition of cooperative activity, but (2) trust, to be effective and stable, depends on being able to rely on other people's dispositions to be sincere and accurate. This nondeontological approach allows Williams to address subtle cases where the general importance of a disposition toward truth can accommodate "social falsehood" (as in some forms of polite "white lies" that sustain the good will necessary for trust itself) or cases where the apparent requirement to speak the truth is overridden by special circumstances (as when a known murderer comes to the door and asks if your children are at home) (2002: 113, 117). For, as Williams points out, "Not everyone … equally deserves the truth," including a person who deals with you outside "the normal expectations of truthful exchange," nor does "everyone [have] a right to know everything" (2002: 117).

Williams demonstrates the valuable flexibility of a broadly ethics-oriented approach in dealing with the complexities that the requirement to tell the truth generates—an important advantage in thinking about the complex issues raised by contemporary media. Williams goes on to discuss what happens to truth-related virtues when applied at the larger scale on which states, politics, and media institutions operate (2002: chapter 9). He demolishes the comforting neoliberal assumption that free media markets ipso facto guarantee the outcomes such as trust (2002: 213–215) that normally are secured by individual truth telling, and suggests that a "free" media system may *not* in fact sustain the wider "complex of attitudes and institutions that as a whole stand against tyranny," even if the absence of uncensored media would bring an increased risk of tyranny. A free press is, in other words, a necessary but far from sufficient condition of freedom and the good life on a large scale, leaving plenty of room for debate about media's necessary virtues. Those institutional implications are not, however, something Williams develops fully.

Avoiding Harm and Enabling Others' Virtue

It is useful here, in an eclectic spirit, to turn to Onora O'Neill's deontological discussion since she pays more attention than Williams to the question of what specific demands we can make of media *institutions*. As a Kantian, O'Neill derives her principles of justice from the Kantian principle of universalizability, indeed that principle's most general form, which is that agents should reject any action that harms others (1996: 161–166). As it happens, that principle is easy enough to fit into a virtue-based framework as well (Williams, 2002: 118), so the interesting question (relevant to both ethical and deontological traditions) is more: what exactly do we mean by "harm"?

O'Neill usefully defines *harm* broadly to include indirect injury to others through damage to "the social connections between agents, and so the conventions, trust, traditions and relationships by which pluralities of agents maintain a social fabric and complex capabilities" (1996: 168). Here too there is no fundamental incompatibility with virtue ethics, which is useful since as we saw in chapter 6 O'Neill goes further than Williams and Lovibond in considering the inequalities inherent in the current organization of media production, not just on a national level, but also on a global level (1996: 170). O'Neill has since developed her arguments against untrammeled media power into a trenchant call for more accountability of media institutions (O'Neill, 2002), an argument on which I will touch below. The force of O'Neill's argument derives, I suggest, *less* from any deontological premises and *more* from her analysis of the damage that an unequal system of communication can cause to freedom. That analysis can be integrated equally well into an account of media ethics.[25] A virtue-based model would also discourage practices that systematically harm others and undermine their capacity for virtue (cf. Williams, 2002: 122); if the truth-related virtues include the acquisition of appropriate levels of knowledge about the world around us (as Lovibond's account of communicative virtue suggests), then an unbalanced or untruthful media is a direct interference with audiences' capacities to develop an accurate picture of the world they live in.

Indeed, we might go further and argue for rethinking media's obligations in terms of a requirement to facilitate each citizen's possibilities of living well. This would move our discussion from issues of ethical action to questions of justice. Strong encouragement for such a move comes from the philosopher and development economist Amartya Sen's work on "human functionings" (Sen 1992), which Nicholas Garnham (1999b) has shown can be powerfully applied in evaluating media performance. Sen aims to move beyond the constraints of rational choice theory in economics by reworking its philosophical foundations in a utilitarian account of the good as discrete goods in one's hand, as it were (Sen, 1992: 6–8). But, Sen argues, since humans have the capacity to choose between goods, we can only assess the good of a life by measuring it against not acquired goods but the fulfillment of human capabilities; even here, since we may freely choose among the capabilities we wish to exercise, we must look not at what one actually does, but at what one has the opportunity to do in fulfillment of one's capabilities. Here Sen uses an Aristotelian concept of human needs to ground the notion of human functionings, which is a proper range of the capabilities (relative to human needs) that a person must at least have the opportunity to exercise if her life is to be considered good. As Sen puts it (1992: 39): "The claim is that functionings are constitutive of a person's being, and an evaluation of well-being has to take the form of an assessment of those constitutive elements."

As Garnham (1999b) was the first to point out, Sen's argument gives us a powerful tool with which to evaluate media performance without passing through the uncertainties of democratic theory, since in any state (whether or not a democracy), we might argue, media should act in such a way as to enhance the functionings of each individual; this must include providing individuals with the information they need to monitor the decisions being taken on matters that affect them; indeed, Sen's arguments (1999) for democracies with a free press as essential for development imply as much. I will not, however, pursue this line of argument further here because to do so would require a broader account of *justice* in relation to media, and raise therefore the question of how society's resources can be distributed fairly between individuals and institutions. For now, let us see how far we can get by relying on a more limited argument, namely, what would constitute virtues for participants in the media process.

Even from the point of view of media's own ethical performance rather than its compliance with a wider notion of justice, we need media institutions to comply with standards of communicative virtue. Media should be accountable for their compliance with ethical standards not because, in failing to do so, they breach a universal moral rule (about what is right or just) but because, if they regularly act unethically, there is good reason to think that a basic feature of our collective and individual life will be damaged.

What principles can we build from these foundations that might be the starting point for a specifically media-focused ethics?

Some Modest Proposals for a Media Ethics

To be clear: the aim here is not to "legislate" for how media institutions should behave. That would be already in conflict with how ethics approaches things. Rather in proposing some principles, I am simply trying to articulate what might be consensual starting points from which more detailed debate on media ethics could develop. Even if these principles do not win consensus, then they should at least provoke debate on what alternative principles might be generally accepted as a basis for discussion.

Nor, of course, do I claim that these principles apply automatically in every space and historical period—their detailed applicability will always depend on practice in specific contexts (cf. Williams, 2002: 34)—although I have deliberately formulated them in quite general terms, in the (perhaps naïve!) hope that they might seem plausible to people across a range of moral, religious, and political frameworks and cultural settings.

The Media's Ethical Responsibility

The ethical principles that I outline shortly all start out from a preliminary point, whose apparent obviousness is regularly obscured in our everyday dealings with media: *that media should be ethically responsible for what they do as should actors in any other area of life.* "But, of course," you might respond, "how could it be otherwise?" Yet most of what media do, including the harm they cause to those represented in their narratives and images, is treated as if it were beyond ethical challenge. As Onora O'Neill has argued in the United Kingdom (but there are many countries, I suggest, where this is also true), media institutions are extraordinarily unaccountable for the detailed consequences of their actions: "The media, in particular the print media—while deeply preoccupied with others' untrustworthiness—have escaped demands for accountability (apart from the financial disciplines set by company law and accounting practices ... [for example] there is no requirement to make evidence [for their judgments and claims] accessible to the readers" (2002: 89–90). This quarantining from sustained ethical inquiry of what all acknowledge to be a significant area of contemporary public life sends out a message of irresponsibility that needs to be challenged.

I am not saying, of course, that every act media perform should be subject to external intervention, whether legal or otherwise, for that would constrain in a dangerous way media's capacity to challenge political and other forms of power (cf. principle 5 under "Defending Press Freedom, Limiting Press License"). Rather, such exceptions as media have from the normal consequences of ethical responsibility must always be justified as *exceptions* to the usual principle that each of us takes the full consequences that flow from our ethical accountability toward others. These exceptions may be something necessary to protect media's acknowledged role in challenging public power, but again only as *purpose-specific* exceptions to the wider rule of ethical responsibility. As Onora O'Neill puts it succinctly: "The press has no licence to deceive us and we have no reason to think that a free press needs such licence" (2002: 100).[26]

This takes us to the question of what the purpose of media is, if seen from an ethical perspective. Many journalists, and indeed the whole U.S. liberal tradition based around the First Amendment, would say media's purpose is to protect people from the state, linking media to a fundamental narrative about democratization. That is an important argument, and one I would want to rely on in many circumstances, but it helps us less here since our aim, in building a framework of media ethics, was to do so *without* recourse to the highly disputed area of political theory. Since it is implausible to expect anything like consensus, or even as yet a shared field of debate, around those issues on a global scale, the wager of a global media ethics is to build its argument from different foundations. As it happens, virtue ethics addresses questions of social purpose from another angle entirely.

It is here that the distance of contemporary virtue ethicists from Aristotle's formulations (hardly sympathetic, as is well known, to democracy!) is greatest. Rosalind Hursthouse (1999: 202) puts the position very clearly when she argues (from within a framework that is explicitly neo-Aristotelian) that whether a person is fit to contribute to the flourishing of their species depends on a four-way understanding of "fitness" in terms of its contribution to "(1) [that person's] individual survival, (2) the continuance of its species, (3) [the person's] characteristic freedom from pain and characteristic enjoyment, and (4) the good functioning of [her] social group—in the ways characteristic of the species." While we might question that word *functioning* (see chapter 2), the idea that virtue, in one of its key dimensions, consists of acting in such a way that the group of which one is part *lives well* is clear. What is that group? In a world of global communications and many other forms of global mobility and transmission, this group today must mean any polity up to and including the world.

In a less abstract setting, the Australian virtue ethicists Oakley and Cocking ask what is the aim of the medical profession, toward which virtuous doctors and nurses should aim (2001: chapter 3); the answer, fairly clearly, is the health of the human body. Without pretending there are any simple analogies between the health of the body and (metaphorically) social life (once again, that would be the functionalist trap), we can still ask, by analogy, what might be the "end" or ultimate aim of media practice that produces information for large social groups up to and including the world's population? What other aim could there be than to provide *accurate* information about the shared circumstances of that group, on the basis of which that group can flourish as human beings, both individually and collectively?

This starting point for virtue ethics, then, involves no appeal to a theory of democracy, although it does, of course, note right away that individuals, groups, and institutions have interests that may conflict with the free flow of information, interests that media in most democracies are expected to contest. To any journalists who resent the claim of virtue ethics to interfere in their practice, there is a straightforward reply: this is the necessary consequence of taking seriously what journalists do, as a distinctive contribution to what Aristotelians would call "human flourishing" (or, we might just say, "living well"). Media comprise a "practice" in the sense of another founder of contemporary virtue ethics, Alisdair MacIntyre (1981: 175), that is, a coherent and complex form of cooperative human activity whose internal goods involve distinctive standards of excellence, which, if achieved, extend our notion of human excellence. Media practice *matters* for how humans flourish more broadly in an era where we depend on the circulation of vast amounts of socially relevant information, and media are vitally involved in that exchange. It follows that a general ethics of media practice is relevant to all of us.

Media's Reflexive Virtues

My first set of principles relate directly to the virtues that we can expect of media institutions. I have already argued that there is no question of excluding media institutions from the ethical standards we would expect of individuals[27]; on the contrary, we can expect specific and additional standards for media, derived from their institutional purpose. What does this entail?

Accuracy and sincerity. The first principle I propose is as follows: *media institutions should aim always to be accurate and sincere* (i.e., to show the two truth-related virtues: cf. Williams, 2002) *and should be ethically accountable, just as individuals are ethically accountable, if they fall short of those virtues.*

Communicative virtues are not optional; reliable practices of truth telling, that is, ethical dispositions to tell the truth are, Bernard Williams argues, essential in any social world, whether explicitly democratic or not. Media institutions, of course, have many immediate goals, just as institutions do, which include making the profits or achieving the public audiences they require for success, whether they operate principally under market constraints or under state license. Those goals may well be legitimate and necessary, if media institutions are to exist at all. But accounts that see media freedom as of primary importance—this, as O'Neill has pointed out (2005), is the traditional account of press freedom from John Stuart Mill (1929)—would not allow any other consideration (such as media ethics) to interfere with the protection of the media's freedoms to satisfy its own ends; of course, media under Mill's model are expected to behave in accordance with their internal ethical standards, like any other institutions, but that remains precisely an *internal* matter. O'Neill has challenged this by arguing that press freedom is not an absolute value and we should not forget the aim for which press freedom is socially endorsed, namely, the sustaining of wider democratic freedom (O'Neill, 2002). Indeed, the logic of most journalists' view of themselves—that media are free in order to protect citizens' freedom from state interference—*requires* that media freedom is conditional on media fulfilling that purpose; if media directly act *against* that purpose, how can we safely allow media to remain free?!

Such arguments (developed forcibly by Onora O'Neill) depend on an account of democratic theory, if they are to work as more than ad hominem challenges to journalists who use democratic theory as their self-defense. For O'Neill, this fits with her wider account of media obligations within an account of justice in democratic societies. However, for reasons already explained, I am seeking here a wider grounding for media ethics that avoids reliance on democratic theory and does not depend on a prior account of justice. Media *ethics* starts from individually focused questions—how should I live and act?—although, as we saw, this quickly opens out onto the social consequences if particular ethical standards are, or are not, adopted by all.

Since media institutions produce accounts of the world that can be true or false, and that imply various other claims about the world, it would be absurd if media were exempt from the truth-related virtues of accuracy and sincerity—absurd, that is, unless the ends for which media act require other virtues that make truth telling irrelevant. As we see, however (principle 2), truth telling is intrinsic to the purpose of media institutions, so doubt about the application of the truth-relative virtues to media does not apply.

How might we expect the virtues of "accuracy" and "sincerity" (discussed in detail by Williams, 2002) to apply to media institutions? Clearly, not in exactly the same way that they apply to private individuals acting outside institutions whose avowed aim is to represent the social world to us. When we expect media *institutions* to be accurate, we are entitled also to expect them to put resources into ensuring that they are accurate, so far as is possible, and into publicly correcting their account, when they know it to have been inaccurate. Clearly, media need resources to generate any stories, but that is not enough; if media institutions are to conform to any plausible standard of truthfulness, we should expect them to apply resources specifically to the checking of stories in advance, and to use those resources well for that purpose. So much is surely uncontroversial.

Another crucial difference that affects what the truth-related virtues mean in practice derives from the scope and range of statements that media make about the world, compared to those made by individuals. As individuals, the statements we make to others about the world are heavily circumscribed in scope and range: on the one hand, by limits on our background knowledge and interpretative resources, and on others' knowledge of those limits; on the other hand, by limits on our access to means of circulating whatever statements we make. Those two types of limits apply in radically different ways to media institutions. As to scope, media comment on *almost everything* going on in the world and there are few recognized limits to the topics on which media are regarded as plausible makers of truth claims (in Britain, at least, the substance of religious belief might be one such limit, but there are few others). The distributional range of media statements varies, of course, depending on which media institution we are discussing, but all media outlets (including small local presses) can, in an age of Web-enhanced journalism, rely on at least the possibility that their stories may be picked up by others and redistributed on a larger scale. Web news sources know their statements can be picked up by anyone from anywhere.

These huge differences in the nature of what private individuals and media institutions are doing when they make claims about the world justify different expectations about the resources that each, if virtuous, should put into ensuring those claims are accurate. Sometimes, we allow individuals to make almost any claim they like, as in friendly banter[28]; generally we expect individuals, unless they are acting in an acknowledged expert or contractual role, to speak on the basis of quite limited sources and attention to accuracy, although there are infinite variations of detail, depending on circumstances and purpose. But with media institutions the situation is completely different. If I found out that a media institution, in making a claim about, say, the implications of a particular government policy, had relied upon the interpretations of three sources who it knew had an interest in presenting that policy in a particular way, would I be likely to be satisfied with that institution's ethical standards? Hardly! Whether we, as readers or viewers, regularly have the information *on which to assess* such matters is open to considerable doubt, but this indicates only how undeveloped debates about media ethics are.

The position is complicated further when we consider what interests media institutions have in telling a story one way, rather than another. Whether it is an individual or an institution doing the telling, *how* a story gets told involves, of course, many variables: what is included and excluded as basic content, which elements are emphasized and which are not, what is presented as a reason for what, what conclusions are reached or not, what sources are explicitly relied upon and which are suppressed, whether the reliability of those sources is explicitly discussed, and so on. It is obvious that agents' interests affect the stories they tell. When dealing with private individuals, we generally allow for this, and discount the claims that others make in various ways, relying on our knowledge of their actual interests (just as we take account of the limits of their knowledge). We make other kinds of allowance for individuals' acting in a professional capacity: we know that the sales person wants us to buy a particular product, or that the lawyer speaking in court is speaking first and foremost in the interests of her client. When dealing with institutions, particularly those such as media whose official purpose is, in part, to *provide* us with significant information, the situation is very different. We may assume a media institution has certain interests—how could it not?—but we are also likely to assume it generally aims to act well in accordance with its general purpose of telling us about things that matter in the world. Since media (unlike individuals) tell us countless different things, there are likely to be very many cases where we simply can't distinguish whether the media institution has interests that might affect how it tells a particular story. Yet those stories may be ones on which we would like to rely.

This is where the second truth-related virtue of sincerity becomes crucial. Williams characterizes "sincerity" as follows: "Sincerity consists in a disposition to make sure that one's assertion expresses what one actually believes" (2002: 96). What this means in practice is complicated because we always communicate more than we believe, since the conventional practices of language involve inferring all sorts of things from the fact that something has been said (or indeed written):

> Hearers gather more from a speaker's making a particular assertion than the content of that assertion ... the speaker expresses one belief, but [the hearers] acquire many. Speakers have countless beliefs and many different ways of expressing them. They could always have said something else, mentioned a different matter, made their statement more or less determinate. The fact that in a given context the speaker says one thing rather than another gives information to the hearer, and this of course is itself a means of communication. Moreover, it is an essential feature of language. There may be special circumstances in which it is understood that a hearer is to ignore everything about an assertion except its content, but they are very special. In general, in relying on what someone said, one inevitably relies on more than what he *said*. (Williams, 2002: 100, original emphasis)

Sincerity then requires the speaker, or the writer, to pay attention to what the recipient is likely to believe as a result of what she says or writes. In the case of an individual, the scope and range of one's truth claims are, as noted, generally rather limited. Not so with media institutions, which means that sincerity on their part is a heavy commitment, although a nonnegotiable one, closely related, as Williams's discussion brings out, to the possibility of anyone's having trust in that institution.

What type of factors might lead one to see a media institution as insincere? First, if it had a specific purpose in telling a story a certain way, which it did not disclose, yet could not expect the audience to know. Second, if it disclosed one purpose in telling a story a certain way, yet in fact had another, contradictory purpose in telling that story. Third, if it presented a story a certain way—knowing that this would lead its audience to make certain inferences—while knowing that those inferences would be false.

Consider now the types of interest that media institutions typically declare as motivating the claims they make about the world: for example, that "the British people need to know this" or that "this is an important story whose truth needed to come out." If media claim such an interest in telling a particular story while having another undisclosed interest in doing so, they are acting insincerely. Or consider the most common clichés of media storytelling: "the American people are angry," or "the British people cannot accept this situation," and so on. Such language implies the media institution has *evidence* that "the people" (whoever they are) do indeed think this or that. Yet a devastating new study by Justin Lewis and colleagues (Lewis, Inthorn, and Wahl-Jorgensen, 2005) shows that claims of this sort (whether in Britain or the United States, whether on television or in the press) are rarely backed by remotely plausible evidence. Unless media institutions believe that no one believes their claims of this nature, then they are falling short of both accuracy and sincerity.

Journalists might object that much media discourse is rhetorical, and known by its audience to be uttered from a specific and *interested* point of view, like that of the lawyer arguing her client's case in court. This would be a reasonable argument if media did not spend so much energy asserting that they stand *above* specific interests! Here it is worth returning to Bernard Williams's detailed characterization of sincerity as a disposition that ensures people can rely on the inferences about others' beliefs that they are required to make in linguistic exchange. Everyday conversation is based on the expectation that "language [operates] under favourable social conditions which enable it to be ... cooperative" (Williams, 2002: 100). Add in the wider purpose of media institutions (discussed shortly), which is to circulate the information necessary for us to live well together, and it becomes clear that:

(1) We have no choice but to make certain assumptions about the sincerity of what media say to us;
(2) If media are insincere in various respects (in the sorts of ways already discussed), this is ethically irresponsible on their part.

There is, of course, much talk about media literacy, and one could at this point turn round and argue that the burden of cautious interpretation lies entirely with the audience (whose [lack of] literacy is their problem). Certainly, sophistication in interpreting media rhetoric should be a basic element of education in a mediated world (just as training in the rhetoric of the court room and the political meeting was in Classical Greece and Rome part of the basic education for those who received formal education!). Yet so far debates about media literacy (more prominent in the United Kingdom since a new regulatory body for media, the Office of Communications (OFCOM), was given the responsibility for promoting it) have taken place without much debate on the levels of accuracy and sincerity that literate media consumers have a right to expect from media!

Note that there is much more to the media's truth-related virtues than factual accuracy; as a result, the media's virtues are relevant to much more than news and documentary. Reality television is an important example of a whole genre whose marketability depends at *some* level (not necessarily the most immediate, referential level, although sometimes here too) on claims being made about the "reality" (i.e., truthful correspondence to some reality) of what is shown (cf. Couldry 2003a, chapter 6). Not only are such claims made, but, as the discussion of sincerity suggests, media can expect that they are relied upon—otherwise, why make them? If media institutions can expect such claims to be acted upon, then the question arises again what basis there is for such claims, and questions of accuracy and sincerity apply, even if in more complex and indirect ways than with news and documentary where facts are continually and directly asserted.

I could go on and discuss the ethics of other areas of contemporary media, for example, celebrity culture. Here, in addition to accuracy and sincerity, other virtues (or vices) less closely related to truth become relevant. It is not obviously virtuous to take pleasure in the embarrassment of others, or to make malicious accusations designed to harm others for your own benefit. Yet this is what media institutions regularly do in celebrity coverage—is this ethical? If so, how? If not, why do we accept it? Pursuing this question, however, would take us too far afield, although it signals the wider areas that a media ethics could open up. Instead, let's focus on why exactly media should pursue accuracy and sincerity.

Media's purpose. Here we can suggest a second principle: *the principal aim toward which media virtues are directed is to circulate information that contributes to the successful individual and collective life of the territory to which they transmit.* In every country, of course, there will be specific debates about the extent to which local media institutions act ethically, judged by this standard. The standard itself, however, is surely "nonnegotiable" (in Bernard Williams's term) since information is always necessary for the conduct of social life. This dimension of the media virtues derives from the particular role that media play in a world where each of us is dependent on others, including institutions that circulate information necessary for our lives together. If such institutions fall short of their virtues at one level (principle 1), media commit what MacIntyre calls an "offence versus truthfulness" at another level, preventing others from learning what they need to learn (1999: 151).

There is also an important point about the *global* context in which such ethical debates must be encouraged. While the frameworks under which media are regulated are to all intents and purposes national, media institutions themselves operate well beyond the confines of the nation-state, covering events (as they have done for centuries) that are global in their implications and increasingly selling their stories and images on global markets. It follows that the scale on which media contribute to our collective life is global as well, and must be assessed on a global scale also. The ethical responsibilities of media institutions are in this respect no different from those of governments, corporations, and nongovernmental organizations (NGOs).

Clearly, we are only at the beginning of understanding the implications of the global dimension for media ethics. At the very least, however, I want to propose that, in a world currently riven by dangerously opposed and apparently incompatible worldviews, we are entitled to expect that media (not just governments, corporations, and other institutions) *act in such a way that promotes dialogue between those worldviews*—not because dialogue is an absolute value (as communitarian ethics assumes), but because *lack* of dialogue and exchange promotes misunderstanding that is likely to be dangerous, whatever our identities and interests. Worse, if media act to stimulate misunderstanding and even hatred among groups, nations, and global religions, as currently often happens, then how can media be said to be acting ethically? It is an open question, for example, whether some North American and UK media coverage of the U.S.-led "war on terror" is ethical by this standard. To the extent that it is not, media cannot expect citizens to endorse automatically the freedom that democracies grant media. At the very least, the ethics of media's current practice must become an issue for regular public debate—and on a scale that allows for a transnational exchange of perspectives.

Media's ethical reflexivity. This connects with a third principle, designed to extend the scope and sensitivity of the virtues that media institutions are expected to maintain: *media institutions should spend sufficient time reflecting on the wider consequences of how they represent our shared world (not only for their own ethical performance, but also for the general living conditions in those territories and, indeed, the world as a whole), and such reflection should be open to public participation.* Media, for example, should consider how they contribute to the terms on which current conflict, whether on a national or a global scale, is constructed. They should consider to what extent they give voice to the full range of opinions in a democracy. These are just some of the questions, many of which no doubt already exercise individual journalists, that media institutions, if they are to be ethical agents, should reflect upon.

This reflexivity needs, in part, to be public for a number of reasons: first, because some degree of public dialogue is necessary for the revival of trust in media, which, as is well known, is in many countries at a low ebb; second, because media ethics is itself a public question, involving all (whether employed in media or not) who contribute to the media process and affecting all citizens, so ethical reflection that excludes the general public is incomplete.

The media's ethical reflection must take place, in part, beyond as well as within media outputs (programs, newspapers); otherwise, it has little chance of obtaining the necessary distance from what it is supposed to be reflecting upon. This requires face-to-face accountability of media professionals to their audiences—a point I return to at the end of the chapter.

The point of these three principles stated so far is not to punish media. (Note that I have talked here about "reflexivity," not "accountability," using the term *accountability* only in the sense of ethical accountability, rather than formal accountability. Questions as to the legal or formal consequences of such reflexivity need to be handled sensitively.) As O'Neill has argued (2002), instituting a paper trail of formal accountability in media institutions that tracks every decision they make is not the way to improve trust in any institution, nor is it the way to promote open dialogue about ethical questions. Public reflection on the benefits as well as the harms committed by media institutions, provided those institutions are willing to reflect on how they live up to the ethical standards appropriate to them, can only strengthen media freedom in the long term, not weaken it.[29]

Defending Press Freedom, Limiting Press License

We do nonetheless need to consider how we should think about the consequences for media institutions if they fall short of ethical standards. It is here that an ethical framework can usefully draw on the deontological tradition, particularly O'Neill's work on "harm." What follows, however, is not a blueprint for new laws or regulations about media but rather a first formulation of principles that might orient us in thinking about the type of legal framework we ultimately need for regulating (where necessary) media practice.

I suggest here a pair of principles, our fourth and fifth.

The fourth principle. *Media should avoid causing harm to individuals who are acting in a private capacity and should be fully and directly responsible to those individuals for any harm they cause, but with the basic defense that the media institution's actions were of a sort that would be normally regarded as fulfilling its own ethical standards (principles 1 and 2).*

This principle follows directly from the principle that it is good/right to avoid causing harm to others. It acknowledges, as Onora O'Neill suggests, that there are many forms of harm (not just physical, but economic and psychological); all of these forms of harm can be inflicted on individuals by media through what they publish. Indeed, the scale and extent of harm media may cause are affected by the repetitions built into what media do: media do not just pass on a story to another person, but to *millions*; this repetition has ethical consequences, since the harm caused to your private life by its becoming "public knowledge" is of a different kind from the harm caused by your friends talking to each other about you.

We need, of course, to acknowledge some countervailing principles that override this general principle in specific cases: for example, since the fact that a person has been *convicted* of a crime is a matter of public record, media must be free to report it and cannot be liable for any resulting damage to the reputation of the criminal. Whether media should always be free to name specific individuals in relation to mere *allegations* of crime is a more difficult matter, which under this principle should be opened up for debate.

This fourth principle is deliberately framed without specific regard for the details of defamation law as it operates in different countries—itself a highly disputed area and one whose limited effectiveness (except for the very rich) is notorious. It should be clear, however, that the harm media can do to individuals (e.g., psychological distress) extends far beyond the damage to what a person can claim as his or her "reputation." Cases where media coverage of a crime and its victim's family intrudes into that family's grief raise difficult, but neglected ethical questions.[30] Defamation law generally involves, it is true, a media exception for "fair comment" where media have reason to believe in the truth of their allegations and those comments concern something of which there is a public need to know. What we mean by a "public need to know" must *itself* be opened up for debate—not necessarily in order to limit it (on the contrary, on clearly public matters concerning governments or corporations, the protection for media comment should arguably be extended: see principle 5) but to clarify its purpose. This is the point of the exception to the fourth principle, and its link to principles 1 and 2 (the ends for which media act).

The notion of a "public" or "social" need to know about the fully legal actions of private individuals acting in a private capacity is surely problematic[31]; yet it is obvious, certainly in the United Kingdom, that a huge amount of such information circulates through media. The public need information that can help them avoid personal harm or exercise more effectively their rights and obligations as citizens; interpersonal gossip, whatever public interest it may generate, does *not* fall within that category, and yet comprises a large proportion of what many media outlets currently cover. Worse, if the 2005 British Press Awards are evidence, the public dissemination of private scandal is regarded as good journalism to be *rewarded*, not criticized (e.g., in 2005, the *News of the World* received the Scoop of the Year award for its front page headline "Beckham's Secret Affair"). Yet within a media ethics framework, we should ask whether such reporting should be legally sanctioned *at all*, not whether it constitutes "best practice"!

This is an area, however, riven with difficult boundary decisions: it is particularly difficult to decide where the protection around private individuals should be drawn, if we are not to prevent that misdeeds in a nonprivate capacity are being inadvertently protected from exposure. But this is precisely my point: we need an *open* debate on these issues, and at the moment we do not have one, because an underlying principle (that media, like any other institution, should be responsible for harm caused to private individuals) has been obscured by the ethical quarantine around media.

The fifth principle. *Media should not be responsible for doing harm to the public reputation of public institutions or private individuals acting in a public capacity, unless media's actions are deliberately or recklessly untruthful or otherwise in serious breach of media's truth-related virtues (principles 1 and 2).* The sharp contrast with the fourth principle is deliberate. Leaving aside the difficult questions of how exactly to draw the line between public behavior (where media need a protected right to report) and private behavior (where media do not need or deserve that right)—which as I said is something that should be opened up to public, and not just expert legal, debate—I am suggesting that media's rights to report on public information should be *strengthened* at the same time as their rights to report on private matters are more strictly controlled.

This can be defended on two independent grounds. First, within an ethical framework, and given the obvious risks and costs of media pursuing complex campaigns to discover what is going on within government or corporations, media institutions, if they are to exercise their capacities to act virtuously, need significant, arguably increased, protection against nonmedia institutions that use defamation laws or other means to block such inquiry. Second, within democratic theory, if the essential contribution of free media is to hold *public* authority to democratic account, then media need increased protection to fulfill this purpose. Or at least this, I suggest, is a general principle on the basis of which citizens, in democracies at least, could openly discuss what type of defamation laws they need.

So I have argued that media should act virtuously, for the ends appropriate to media institutions, and reflect publicly on the degree to which they do so. Where they fail (either by acting for an end that should not be theirs, as in circulating scandal of no public benefit that harms private individuals, or by acting for a good end but without sufficient regard to media's specific virtues, for example, a vendetta against a corporation or government department that is insufficiently based in fact), then media should be responsible for the harm they cause according to legal mechanisms on whose principles we need fresh debate.

Citizens and Nonmedia Institutions in the Media Process

An important implication of the principles just outlined is that they impose burdens not just on media institutions but on all of us. Any of us can be harmed by how media institutions exercise their freedoms (hence principle 4); but equally any of us, whether individually or in groups, can contribute to the media process and so become involved in the harms or benefits media create, and in the degree to which they maintain high ethical standards. If, as I argued at the beginning of the chapter, media ethics is a matter of concern to all citizens, then citizens *themselves* have an ethical responsibility for the media process, insofar as they contribute to that process.

This is important because many such individuals and nonmedia institutions regularly seek to intervene in the media process, by being the source of media stories: from "kiss-and-tell" informants who reveal the sexual exploits of others to governments and commercial corporations that seek to manage their public image. Indeed, unless media had sources outside the media, there would be little news! It follows that, if media virtues contribute to people's living well together, then private citizens and nonmedia institutions need to think about the ethical standards they *themselves* maintain when contributing to media. This point, however, is generally obscured by seeing media ethics as the exclusive concern of media professionals.

Institutions

Let us take institutions first. A long-running political issue in Britain in recent years has been the alleged culture of "spin" surrounding the New Labour government. Since this issue is often pushed by the government's political and media opponents, the issue is in part a purely internal dispute within the media/political circles where government representatives daily deal with journalists and generate the news agenda. But it has raised wider concerns—and quite reasonably—since if a large part of governmental energies are devoted to generating "events" that will play well in media, rather than to the process of government itself, then that is a distortion of the purpose of government.

There are resonances here with long-term debates in the United States about the increasingly constructed and artificial nature of media coverage of the political process (see, for example, Troy, 1991); particular controversy has arisen over the uses of media by the current Bush administration (cf. Giroux, 2004a). Indeed, the issue of the interpenetration of media and political cultures is an issue for many democracies (Meyer, 2002); it emerges, for example, in different terms in countries that are nominally democracies but where media are subject to more or less direct capture by state or corporate interests, such as in Russia (Sattuc, 2004). The issue then of media's appropriate relationship to political and other powerful actors is of wide relevance.

The problems with spin relate specifically to the virtues of truthfulness. For just as individuals do not conform with the virtue of truthfulness by devoting most of their energies to creating the *impression* of acting well rather than acting well, so too for institutions including governments. Once again, the point is not to resolve such issues—it is not easy to say exactly how much of their energies governments in large, complex, multiparty democracies should be devoting to securing a favorable presentation of their actions. It is just such complexity and uncertainty that signal this as an issue for *ethical* discussion, rather than moral fiat: ethical discussion among media professionals, institutions, and citizens. The aim of media ethics should be to encourage the reflexivity of all parties to the media process, not only media professionals.

A very different sort of issue arises where governments, instead of working through the media apparatus, are directly hostile to the existence of media, constraining their operations by laws, licensing constraints and the use of patronage power where the resources for making media are themselves scarce. What use, we might ask, is the ethical sensibility of journalists when in poor countries the only way they can afford to travel to their sources is via transport provided by that source?[32] Once again, however, this takes us into areas of social justice and democratic theory, since ensuring some basic level of funding for media institutions in conditions of scarcity is, arguably, necessary in any democracy.

Private Individuals

The involvement of private individuals in the media process often raises considerable ethical problems. Recall Onora O'Neill's principle: "The press has no licence to deceive us and we have no reason to think that a free press needs such licence" (O'Neill, 2002: 100). Two further principles follow from its opening clause, when considered in relation to nonmedia contributors to the media process: first, that no person or institution outside the press has license to deceive us through the medium of the press; and, second, that the press have no license to encourage any person or institution to deceive us through their medium.

It follows that the frequent practice of media's *paying* sources for their stories is unethical, and for more than one reason. When media pay a source to tell its story to them so that the media outlet can reproduce it, they are either paying the source to tell the truth or paying while not caring whether it tells the truth; this is unethical on the part of media institutions either because (in the first case) they are encouraging the source to act unethically or (in the second case) they are acting without concern for their own ethical standards. Needless to say, if the source accepts money to tell a story whose untruth they know or about whose untruth they are reckless, they too are acting unethically. In other spheres of life, paying someone to do what they are already expected or obliged to do is in most circumstances regarded as bribery; at the very least it is unethical, if not, in many cases, illegal. The dangerous consequences for social life if bribery becomes the norm (so that truth is assumed to be buyable) are obvious, so why do we tolerate what is effectively a culture of bribery in the media sphere, operating under cover of the public's right to know?

It is possible, of course, that in some, perhaps many, cases, sources are paid for stories that are nonetheless true. But the risk that payment will disrupt the source's judgment is so obvious that we can reasonably argue it contradicts the ethical standards we should expect of institutions (media) who are licensed to tell the truth about our world. Arguably, media payments to sources are a sufficient threat to the truthfulness and plausibility of the media process that they should not only be regarded as unethical, but formally prevented by regulation. This does not happen at present, although the issue has been considered and rejected, for example, by the UK Press Complaints Commission (Keeble, 2001: 39–41). Once again, this is an area where media ethics can open up a debate, aimed not at undermining media freedom but encouraging media to concentrate their resources on stories of greater public importance where sources do not need financial incentives to speak.[33] This debate is only made more urgent by the increasing "adoption" of citizens into media production by media's use of mobile phone photos, camcorder footage, and the like.

Rethinking the Process of Media Regulation

So far in this chapter, I have argued for some basic principles that might serve as a consensual starting point for dialogue about media ethics, on both a national and a global scale. These are open principles, designed to aid public discussion on questions whose details will inevitably be contentious, rather than rules that aim to legislate for media practice.

However open and modest these principles are, I must still say something, finally, about the institutional contexts where debate about media ethics might be established. For it is here, at the institutional hurdle, that Tocqueville implied all proposals for a media ethics must fall! "If any one could point out an intermediate, and yet a tenable position, between the complete independence [of the press] and the entire subjection of the public expression of opinion, I should perhaps be inclined to adopt it; but the difficulty is to discover this position" (de Tocqueville, 1964: 204–205). De Tocqueville could find no intermediate position between total media freedom and the suppression of public opinion; on the face of it, there is no institution to enforce standards of media ethics except the state—the very institution against whose threat to freedom the counterpower of free media institutions is, on most accounts, designed to protect us. Is there a way beyond this old impasse?

It is no way out to say that media ethics must (like personal ethics) be a matter for the private conscience of individual journalists. For the *point* of media ethics is to identify areas where media practice can be adjusted in response to open debate, as part of the healthy working of public institutions. Indeed, it is absurdly optimistic to believe that media corporations will simply allow individual journalists to follow their ethical conscience when this conflicts with the need to sell a story under pressure; yet it is absurdly naïve to trust governments, of their own initiative, to set up a regulatory framework at arm's length from the state that could effectively monitor the ethical standards of media institutions and those (in government) who interact with media.

We need therefore to imagine a different starting point. Media ethics is, after all, a major issue for democracy and remedying its suppression is a long-term task of democratic reform. Imagining an institutional basis for debating media ethics is part of imagining—from an imperfect starting point—what Raymond Williams called the "full democratic process" (Williams, 1958: 318). How might we construct ways in which media ethics could over time become a focus of open negotiation between citizens? If actual institutional forms are at present hard to envisage, the *principle*—that the media's ethical standards should be open to regular public scrutiny and challenge by citizens themselves in direct interaction[34] with the representatives of media institutions—is one we can assert right away. It involves, in part, rethinking media regulation so that we see it as part of a deliberative process open to citizen involvement, at least as much as it is a formal process overseen by the state and administered by experts.

Clearly, it is impracticable to open out to public participation every media decision with ethical implications–so too with political decisions and corporate decisions. On the other hand, where there is a "dissociation of public discussion and underlying issues of public concern" (Mayhew, 1997: 236), trust in institutions is likely to be undermined. Leon Mayhew's proposals for how, in the domain of politics, institutional trust might be revived are useful also, by extension, to media practice. Just as Mayhew argues that citizens need the opportunity to "redeem" (i.e., test out) the rhetorical claims about politics face-to-face with the persons who made them, so too citizens need opportunities where they can redeem the rhetorical claims made both explicitly and implicitly by media institutions.

Yet where, for example, can newspaper readers effectively "redeem" newspaper claims that they act in order to satisfy the public's right to know? At present, nowhere effectively (cf. Pritchard, 2000, on the U.S. press). But we can envisage the creation of a network of fora where media professionals could be challenged directly on the substance of such rhetoric and also where broader questions of media ethics might be discussed face-to-face between media professionals and citizens. To be useful, such fora should give citizens the chance not just to *talk* about problems of media ethics (talking is not enough) but also to be satisfied that such deliberations will be taken into account in media's future decision making—which implies some reliable mechanism for media representatives reporting back on action taken. There need to be many such fora at local, regional, and national levels, where representatives of media institutions meet face-to-face with audience members and listen to their concerns. It may be we have to look to societies in crisis or intense development, such as Argentina and India, for examples of how regular face-to-face communication between journalists and social actors can take place.[35]

More radically, the very nature of each media outlet (whether a newspaper, a television channel, or a news-based Web site or Web portal) needs to be rethought of as not just an outlet for news transmission but as a public space where the social world is constructed. If so, then each media outlet should allow, *as a significant part of its output* (through program sections, special pages, and so on), for space where open debate on the ethics of that media outlet can occur. Recent models of Web-based interfaces and discussion fora are potentially useful in leading the way here, although Web fora need always to be redeemable in face-to-face meetings, if they are to be credible over the long term.

Yet, as the Australian journalist Margo Kingston points out (2004), almost all media stand currently opposed to opening up such a public space within their products. We are all familiar with the imbalance between the misleading front-page news story and the two-line apology days later tucked away on the paper's page 25, once the truth of the headline has been successfully challenged. What more obvious sign could there be of media's indifference to their own ethical responsibility? Instead, we should expect all media outlets to print or broadcast responses received by them to their coverage, with responses that successfully challenge its truth taking up a comparable amount of space to that of the original coverage. If they don't do this, media should answer the charge that, in failing to do so, they act unethically.

Chapter 7

Conclusion

It is time to recall why the effort of building a framework for debating media ethics matters. It matters for democracy: there can therefore be no "full democratic process" (in Raymond Williams's term) until the unaccountability of the media process is seriously addressed, not treated as an inconvenient obstruction to media's business as usual. Closing down such discussion (as is currently the norm) is a closure performed against democracy.

But the problem goes deeper. Just as democracy itself matters as a means to something broader (Sen calls it "development"; we might say, even more broadly, our chances of living well, both individually and together), so too does media ethics. For ethics is a shared necessity, not simply an individual obligation, when *in spite of* our profound and mutually obvious differences, all of us "by virtue of [our] common ownership of the earth's surface" (Kant, 1983: 118) must find a way of living well together. Since media are the principal means through which the world's realities are presented, media ethics is a necessity, whether within existing democracies or as a precondition for any of us to live safely in today's interconnected world. But media ethics, like all ethics, starts from where we find ourselves, not from where we would like to be. Ethics is a framework for building consensus, even where none seems available; without it, as Williams said of a common culture, we shall not survive. This is why, in perhaps this book's most controversial move, I have *not* based this chapter's framework for media ethics on specific values that I hold dear (an effective democracy, secularism). It is not that these values are suspended, or reduced in importance (far from it), but rather that we need to find some *other* basis for building consensus, when consensus, at least on a global scale, is precisely lacking. To return to this book's guiding metaphor, it is as if we must stop speaking only in the terms we ourselves prefer and know best, in order to open up a space where we can hear others with whom we may on some things profoundly disagree but with whom we may share at least a commitment to the greater value (abstract, of course, until through dialogue we articulate it further) of living well together. It is this that media must help us do, which requires an evaluative framework to which it is open to everyone affected by media to contribute. If we are ever, any of us and in whatever form, to act as citizens of the world, we need reliable knowledge of its realities, and so we need an ethics that applies to the institutions on which in large measure we rely for that knowledge. This, finally, is where the themes of knowledge, agency, and ethics of chapter 2 intersect.

Where should we be debating media ethics? The fact that, because of its difficulty and the profound silence in which this subject has been shrouded for too long, we started from a *theoretical* discussion does not mean media ethics can be confined to theory. That would be a disaster. The role of theory is simply to find a way—quietly, persistently, against a number of complex resistances—of starting to speak, breaking the silence, and opening up a conversation in which over time all citizens are free to join—not just those who are officially citizens but also those who beyond the limits of formal states have a stake in the establishment of a fairer world where their rights to security and freedom might be respected.

The debate over media ethics is a conversation for many occasions and places; I have already argued that media practice should become more open to such discussions with those who aren't journalists: not as a way of attacking media, but as a way of enhancing its contribution to democracy. Equally, media ethics should become part of what we discuss in schools and universities, not just as a technical requirement for budding media professionals but as an issue that concerns all citizens and all who would be citizens.

Media ethics' required place in the curriculum is not accidental. For if, returning to Paulo Freire (1985), education is based on the value of "experience," then education requires attention to the frameworks within which we might understand better what it is to interact well with each other, as if we genuinely valued their experience. Ethics, and media ethics, would explore what it is like to build on that principle, yet not hold back from the difficult task of articulating through debate what it means to be the type of people who *can* live well together. This is not a conversation we can have, of course, without recalling what in chapter 5 I called the "deformations" of the political, the constraints under which in today's democracies people's experiences come, or do not come, to "count" for others.

It is here that a key value of democracy—listening to others who, as Williams put it, have started from somewhere other than where we have—re-emerges as a value that informs the *practice* of doing media ethics, confirming that the values of democracy are not separate from media ethics, only put to a different, and more indirect, use in its articulation.

In the space of this chapter, I have, of course, far from exhausted the evaluative issues raised by media. Because it would have complicated things too much, I have avoided the question of what justice might be in relation to the distribution of, and access to, the resources of media production: we discussed the problem but not the solution in chapter 6. Justice in media would require a major shift in the way media are organized; this needs separate discussion.[36] Laying some foundations for a media ethics—both as a theoretical framework and as a starting point for everyday civic and educational discussion—has been quite enough of a task. This chapter, I hope, has made at least a small step in that direction.

Notes

1. See, for example, Bertrand (2000) for international overview.

2. This chapter was largely completed before I came across Clifford Christians' recent review of "ethical theory in communications research" (Christians, 2005). There is common ground between the account here and that of Christians, in arguing that a major current challenge for media ethics is "globalizing it" (Christians, 2005: 3) and that, broadly speaking, the ultimate test for media is "do they … contribute to human well-being as a whole?" (2005: 12). But I would argue that Christians, by ignoring the Aristotelian tradition of ethics, makes things unnecessarily difficult, at the same time (ironically) as he echoes Aristotelian thinking (see second quotation from Christians just given). It is not satisfactory to treat the ancient Greek philosophical tradition as if it were homogeneous or, as Christians puts it, damned because "prejudiced to a conceptual Logos" (2005: 8), since this elides the crucial differences between Platonic (indeed, also Kantian) approaches to ethics and Aristotelian, on which see later in the chapter (section on "ethics, not deontology"). Ironically again, the language Christians uses to express his tentative new view of a global ethics that can challenge the "rationalist" tradition (he writes of "the power of the imagination to give us an *inside* perspective on reality": 2005: 8, added emphasis) echoes the language of a recent defense of the ethical tradition derived from Aristotle: "[with] the concept of the virtuous person … [the] conception of right conduct is grasped, as it were, from the inside out" (Macdowell, 1998: 50). Most importantly, the Aristotelian tradition works not through discovery of new "values" (where Christians, rightly, sees so many problems in developing a communication ethics on a global scale) but through rethinking the bases on which ethical debate proceeds. My disagreement with Christians is therefore sharp in the short term but in the long term easily overcome.

3. Cohen-Almagor (2001) speaks as if the only relevant values here were "liberal values." The term *liberal* is quite often used as a catch-all for consensual values, there apparently being no alternative framework for evaluating social and political organization. Although this chapter does not claim to be an essay in political theory, I need to touch on its implicit position within the highly contested field of political theory later on; insofar as its argument depends on taking such a position, its position is republican rather than liberal, although a republicanism with an emphasis on the removal of power inequalities (cf. Pettit, 1999) rather than incorporation into the state.

4. For critical commentary by MediaWise, an important lobbying group in this area, see Cookson and Jempson (2004) and for Weblink http://www.mediawise.org.uk/display_page.php?id=714.

5. See http://www.ijnet.org/FE_Article/codeethics.asp?UILang=1&CId=158650&CIdLang=1 Thanks to Brenda Zulu for alerting me to this development.

6. For a pioneering formulation of the ethics of alternative journalism, see Atton (2003).

7. For example (Christians, Ferré, and Fackler, 1993: 194–195): "We are governed not by autonomous rationality, but by what we love most with our whole heart as whole persons."

8. Cf. the distinction between "normative ethics" and "political philosophy" in Hursthouse (1999: 5–7).

9. Note that the starting point for Aristotle is *not* the concept of virtue but the concept of good, that is, the good life for humankind; there are, of course, other ways of thinking about virtues than this, whether as social requirements or as means to other ends (cf. MacIntyre, 1981: 172–173 for discussion of this point).

10. For a very useful characterization of what is distinctive about virtue ethics, see Oakley and Cocking (2001: chapter 1).

11. I leave out the third, and until recently, quite dominant alternative to deontology, utilitarianism. For a useful discussion of the fault lines and gradual convergence between all three, see Hursthouse (1999: 1–5) and Crisp (1996). For the first, and classic, diagnosis of this fault line, see Anscombe (1997) (originally published in 1958).

12. There are other approaches to virtue ethics that frame it quite differently in terms of common understandings about what count as good motivations in human beings (Slote, 2001). In what follows, I keep to the neo-Aristotelian approach (for a discussion of the difference and also the complex varieties of neo-Aristotelian positions within virtue ethics, see Oakley and Cocking, 2001: 15–17).

13. More fundamentally, the Kantian Barbara Herman argues that "the canon that sorts all moral theories as deontological or teleological" is misleading in the case of Kant, whose ethics, she argues, is *not* deontological, but based in the value of the "good will" (1993: chapter 10). But this is the majority opinion.

14. Thanks to Pete Simonson for making this point forcefully when I presented a version of this chapter at the 2005 International Communication Association (ICA) conference in New York.

15. For example, this passage: "The virtues of political cooperation that make a constitutional regime possible are, then, very great virtues ... the virtues of tolerance and being ready to meet others half-way, and the virtue of reasonableness, and the sense of fairness. When these virtues are widespread in society ... they constitute a very great public good ... thus, the values that conflict with the political conception of justice and its sustaining virtues may normally be outweighed because they come into conflict with the very considerations that make fair social cooperation possible on footing of mutual respect" (Rawls, 1996: 157).

16. For a different balance in approaching this problem, see Silverstone (forthcoming).

17. I say "closer to" because Bernard Williams rejects "naturalism" entirely as the basis of virtue ethics, although Lovibond's and Macdowell's historicist account of "nature" (which includes a "second nature" developed through rational reflection and adaptation) is rather different from the Aristotelian teleology to which Williams objects. See Hursthouse (1999: chapter 10) for a helpful discussion of the issues here.

18. Let alone Levinas's fierce philosophy of obligation based on a primordial "ontology of difference": for criticisms of Levinas, see Ricoeur (1992: 189–190, 337–340); Lovibond (2002: 174–179). There is no space here to discuss fully why I do not find Levinas's work productive as an alternative route beyond the limits of Kant's search for a purely rational grounding of morality. Put briefly, Levinas's ethics seems to reproduce the very absolutism of philosophical formulation that

it seeks to overcome and so detach us from the open-ended process of discursive exchange through which new ethical formulations and understanding might be achieved (cf. chapter 5). Aristotelian naturalism, by contrast, *provided* it is separated from Aristotle's own belief in a fixed, gendered, raced human nature, offers a model of ethical inquiry that, while not making "reason" absolute, does not abandon its capacity to generate understanding either (cf. chapter 4, note 3).

19. For a similar argument about the necessary historical dimension to virtuous practice, see MacIntyre (1981: 180–181).

20. It is here that a reconciliation between "Anglo-American" and poststructuralist philosophy becomes possible, very different in spirit from Rorty's at first inspirational escape into relativism nearly three decades ago (Rorty, 1979). For Lovibond, Williams, and, as we have seen, Ricoeur all draw on poststructuralist thought, while seeking to maintain some continuity with earlier Western moral philosophy. In this perspective, poststructuralism is no longer seen as an absolute break in philosophical history, and Williams's (2002) use of the term *genealogy* for his account of the truth-related virtues can plausibly be a reference to Foucault that is respectful, not ironic. Again, see chapter 4, note 3, on my use of the term *ethics of deconstruction*.

21. For some writers, of course, it is precisely the openness of virtue ethics that is its weakness in supplying guidance on detailed moral questions, as Oakley and Cocking (2001: 31–33) note, and for an example of this in the media ethics field, see Day (2004: 62).

22. See Lovibond (2002: 78, note 33) and compare Aristotle *Nicomachean Ethics* (1976, Book Four). In fact, Lovibond's discussion directly contradicts the spirit of what Aristotle says about justice, since in his discussion of friendship he argues that an act becomes less unjust the further away those affected by it (1976: 273–274). For some, this is a fundamental problem with the Aristotelian approach, requiring alternative sources for virtue ethics (Slote, 2001, looks to eighteenth-century English moral philosophy and twentieth-century feminist writings on the ethics of care). But, leaving aside the special difficulties of the question of justice, Foot's notion of habitat or environment, if made historically sensitive, can surely take account of the global space of interconnectedness in which many contemporary actions, especially those of media, operate.

23. The virtue of truthfulness is treated also in Onora O'Neill's broadly Kantian account as one of a number of "virtues of justice" (along with fairness, toleration, and respect for others) (1996: 187).

24. A similar point emerges in Williams's argument against moral sceptics who doubt that truth telling is generally in the individual's interest (2002: chapter 5).

25. Note also that there is no reason to assume that O'Neill's arguments are available only within a *liberal* theory of democracy: Philip Pettit's version of republicanism offers rather similar suggestions (Pettit, 1999: 167–169).

26. Ignoring this was the error of Belsey and Chadwick, discussed at the beginning of the chapter, when they said (1992: 9) that certain types of sanction against media for unethical behavior (such as closing media operations down) are automatically ruled out by democratic principles. On the contrary, if, as many (including Belsey and Chadwick) argue, media are granted special status in order to protect their role of preserving democracy, then we cannot say, when media are *not* contributing to sustaining democracy, that it would be undemocratic to make them accountable for that failure!

27. I must leave to one side here the difficult, but more specific, question of the level at which responsibility for unethical behavior in media institutions should be primarily regulated: should it be on individual journalists or on the corporate institution? The answer must depend on our views of the power structures within media institutions, but I do not have space to discuss this here.

28. Aristotle discusses this, in a rare discussion of the question of truthfulness in his *Ethics* (1976: 167–168).

29. Compare the insightful and refreshingly open discussion by the Australian journalist Margo Kingston (2003) about the value of discussing freely with readers via her Web site the ethical issues raised from time to time by her work.

30. Cohen-Almagor's discussion explores a number of interesting cases where the consequences of media coverage raise ethical problems, yet could not be addressed in defamation law (Cohen-Almagor, 2001: 95, 97, 100).

31. The very use of the terms *public* and *private*, of course, open a huge controversy. The public/private distinction is one of the most disputed areas of political theory (Kumar and Weintraub, 1997; Geuss, 2001). For some (and I put myself in this camp), this remains the foundation stone of political life (see Elshtain, 1997, for an excellent defense); for others, it is profoundly misleading (Warner, 2002) or at least confusing (Geuss, 2001) in the wake of challenges made by feminism, queer theory, and others. Clearly, I cannot deal with this huge question here.

32. Thanks to Brenda Zulu, a journalist from Zambia, for this comment (e-mail correspondence July 28, 2004).

33. Providing sources with protection, perhaps even financial protection, against the consequences of their speaking out is a different matter.

34. I emphasize "direct *interaction*" to avoid the pitfall analyzed by Onora O'Neill (2002) whereby formal accountability aimed at distant audiences and regulators leads to excessive, rather than meaningful, disclosure that in the longer run undermines trust and the possibility of genuine accountability.

35. For inspiring examples of organizations that are linking civil society and journalists, see http://www.lavaca.org (Argentina) and http://www.voicesforall. org (India), both organizations being linked to the OurMedia/Nuestros Medios network. For that network generally, see http://www.ourmedianet.org.

36. See Gross, Katz, and Ruby (1988) for important work on "image ethics" and the ethics of representation, particularly of sexual and other minorities. See also Couldry and Curran (2003) on justice issues in relation to alternative, nonmainstream media. In thinking about the justice of the media environment, parallels with our ethical responsibilities for the environment via a model of ecology may be useful: cf. Feintuck (1999); Mueller (2004).

Postscript

෴

Media and cultural research have contributed much to the "depth"[1] of our understanding of the social world: exploring the logic of the media production system that lies behind the most available representations of the social world, exploring the open-ended variety of what people make of, or do with, those representations, enriching our understanding of how individuals do, or don't, fit within media's and other constructions of "culture."

In this book, I have suggested some further ways in which media and cultural research might deepen our social understanding when in many parts of the world some believe the very fabric of the social world is unraveling: through asking how media contribute to people's sense of agency across their work and leisure lives; through asking what possibilities for agency people have in relation to systems of representative democracy whose scope, scale, and purpose no longer seem to mesh with the prevalent conditions of everyday life; and finally, by asking whether we can build a framework within which media's ethical implications can be articulated and challenged.

No synoptic view of these different explorations is possible; each started from a different place and encountered different frictions along the way. Some chapters operated under the sign of media research, others under the sign of cultural studies, and in the final two chapters we set out without any clear disciplinary badge but with the aim of stimulating debate about media ethics within and beyond the academy. Precise disciplinary labels (the term *cultural studies* perhaps being most in dispute) matter less here than the motivating values: a resistance to reducing the complexity of the social world when representing it; a concern with the preconditions for achieving the reality (not just the illusion) of an inclusive democracy; a concern with power in all its guises but particularly (because most relevant to media and culture and also often neglected) the consequences of concentrations of symbolic power, especially for those who are not their direct beneficiaries.

Those values are not exclusive to media and cultural studies, but they fit well there, perhaps better than anywhere else. This is a research tradition that may be entering a new phase from which we can reinterpret the doubts of the past decade as the uncertainty that precedes any paradigm shift.

With the increasing rationalization of academic life, the idea of stopping in the midst of the flow of contemporary culture and listening out for different links and understandings may seem counterintuitive. After all, it slows us down, questions our assumptions, values not the speed of production but the time needed for reflecting, revisiting, reformulating—time that so often we do not have and certainly cannot "account for." This is not "fast knowledge," to use Besley and Peters's (2005) phrase from their critique of the contemporary university.

I have tried to keep in mind, while knowing I could not adequately deal with its complexities, the current—dangerous and anxious—global political context. We have learned enough, I hope, along the way to make our relationship to a mediated world, whether as researchers, citizens, or ethical agents, just a little more manageable.

If so, we are ready to start walking back toward the roar of the traffic.

Note

1. We sometimes, informally, think of the social world in terms of depth: various levels of order, deep structures, a move in our analysis from surface to depth. This notion rests, of course, on a metaphor, since our sense of what lies below or behind the surface presented to us depends on an understanding of plausible causal relations that is constructed, and specific to historically shifting research paradigms, not universal. Yet it remains difficult to do without the metaphor of depth.

References

~❧~

Abercrombie, N., and Longhurst, B. 1998. *Audiences: A Sociological Theory of Performance and Imagination.* London: Sage.

Abercrombie, N., et al. 2000. *Penguin Encyclopedia of Sociology.* 4th ed. Penguin: Harmondsworth.

Abercrombie, N., Hill, S., and Turner, B. 1981. *The Dominant Ideology Thesis.* London: Allen and Unwin.

Abu-Lughod, L. 1999. "The Interpretation of Culture(s) after Television," in S. Ortner, ed., *The Fate of "Culture": Geertz and Beyond.* Berkeley: University of California Press.

Adams, T. 2005. "He Shall Not, He Shall Not Be Moved." *Observer,* 24 July 2005, p. 4.

Alasuutaari, P., ed. 1999. *Rethinking the Media Audience.* London: Sage.

Albrow, M. 1997. "Travelling Beyond Local Cultures: Socioscapes in a Global City," in J. Eade, ed., *Living the Global City.* London: Routledge.

Almond, G., and Verba, S. 1963. *The Civic Culture: Political Attitudes and Democracy in Five Nations.* Princeton, NJ: Princeton University Press.

d'Ancona, M. 2005. "Blair Proves Equal to the Long-Dreaded Day." *Sunday Telegraph,* 10 July 2005, p. 23.

Anderson, P. 2005. "Arms and Rights." *New Left Review* 31: 5–46.

Ang, I. 1996. *Living Room Wars.* London: Routledge.

Anscombe, E. 1997 [1958]. "Modern Moral Philosophy," in R. Crisp and M. Slote, eds., *Virtue Ethics.* Oxford: Oxford University Press.

Appadurai, A. 1990. "Disjuncture and Difference in the Global Cultural Economy," in M. Featherstone, ed., *Global Cultures.* London: Sage.

Arendt, H. 1958. *The Human Condition.* Chicago: University of Chicago Press.

References

Aristotle. 1976. *Nicomachean Ethics*. Trans. J. Thomson, rev. H. Tredennick. Penguin: Harmondsworth.

Atton, C. 2001. *Alternative Media*. London: Sage.

Atton, C. 2003. "Ethical Issues in Alternative Journalism." *Ethical Space: The International Journal of Communication Ethics* 1(1): 26–31.

Baker, C. E. 2002. *Media, Markets, and Democracy*. Cambridge: Cambridge University Press.

Balibar, E. 2004. *We, the People of Europe? Reflections of Transnational Citizenship*. Princeton: Princeton University Press.

Barber, B. 1984. *Strong Democracy: Participatory Politics for a New Age*. Berkeley: University of California Press.

Barker, M., and Brooks, K. 1998. *Knowing Audiences*. London: Routledge.

Barnett, C. 2003. *Culture and Democracy*. Edinburgh: Edinburgh University Press.

Barthes, R. 1972. *Mythologies*. London: Paladin Books.

Baudrillard, J. 1983. *Simulations*. New York: Semiotext(e).

Bauman, Z. 1987. *Legislators and Interpreters*. Cambridge: Polity.

Bauman, Z. 1992. *Postmodern Ethics*. Oxford: Blackwell.

Bauman, Z. 1999. *In Search of Politics*. Cambridge: Polity.

Bauman, Z. 2001. *The Individualised Society*. Cambridge: Polity.

Bausinger, H. 1984. "Media, Technology, and Daily Life." *Media, Culture, and Society* 694: 343–352.

BBC. 2002. *Beyond the Soundbite: BBC Research into Public Disillusion with Politics*. London: BBC. Available from www.trbi.co.uk/trbipolitics.pdf (accessed 9 August 2004).

Beck, U. 1992. *Risk Society*. London: Sage.

Beck, U. 1997. *The Reinvention of Politics*. Cambridge: Polity.

Beck, U. 2000a. "The Cosmopolitan Perspective: Sociology of the Second Age of Modernity?" *British Journal of Sociology* 51(1): 79–105.

Beck, U. 2000b. *What Is Globalization?* Cambridge: Polity.

Belsey, A., and Chadwick, R. 1992. "Ethics and Politics of the Media: The Quest for Quality," in Belsey, A., and Chadwick, R., eds., *Ethical Issues in Journalism and the Media*. London: Routledge.

Benhabib, S., ed. 1996. *Democracy and Difference*. Princeton: Princeton University Press.

Benjamin, J. 1998. *Shadow of the Other*. New York: Routledge.

Benjamin, W. 1968 [1936]. "The Storyteller," in *Illuminations*. New York: Schocken Books.

Bennett, L. 1998. "The Uncivic Culture: Community, Identity, and the Rise of Lifestyle Politics." *PS: Political Science and Politics* 31(4): 740–761.

Bennett, T. 1998. *Culture: A Reformer's Science*. London: Sage.

Bertrand, C.-J. 2000. *Media Ethics and Accountability Systems*. New Brunswick: Transaction.

Besley, T., and Peters, M. 2005. "The Theatre of Fast Knowledge: Performative Epistemologies in Higher Education." *Review of Education, Pedagogy, and Cultural Studies* 27: 111–126.

Bhabha, H. 1994. "DissemiNation: Time, Narrative, and the Margins of the Modern Nation," in *The Location of Culture*. London: Routledge.

Bird, S. E. 2003. *The Audience in Everyday Life: Living in a Media World*. London: Routledge.

Bloch, M. 1989. *Ritual History and Power*. London: Athlone Press.

Blumenberg, H. 1987. "An Anthropological Approach to the Contemporary Significance of Rhetoric," in K. Baynes et al., eds., *After Philosophy: End or Transformation?* Cambridge, MA: MIT Press.

Boltanski, L. 1999. *Distant Suffering*. Cambridge: Cambridge University Press.

Bourdieu, P. 1977. *Outline of a Theory of Practice*. Cambridge: Cambridge University Press.

Bourdieu, P. 1990. *Language and Symbolic Power*. Cambridge: Polity.

Bourdieu, P. 1998. *Acts of Resistance*. London: Pluto.

Bourdieu, P. et al., 1999. *The Weight of the World*. Cambridge: Polity.

Bourdieu, P. 2000. *Pascalian Meditations*. Palo Alto, CA: Stanford University Press.

Boyd-Barrett, O. 1977. "Media Imperialism," in J. Curran et al., eds., *Mass Communications and Society*. London: Open University Press.

Boyd-Barrett, O. 1998. "Media Imperialism Reformulated," in D. Thussu, ed., *Electronic Empires*. London: Arnold.

Boyd-Barrett, O., and Rantanen, T., eds. 1998. *The Globalisation of News*. London: Sage.

Brunsdon, C., and Morley, D. 1978. *Everyday Television: Nationwide*. London: BFI.

Buckingham, D. 2000. *The Making of Citizens*. London: Routledge.

Buck-Morss, S. 2003. *Thinking Past Terror: Islamism and Critical Theory on the Left*. London: Verso.

Butler, J. 1993. *Bodies That Matter*. New York: Routledge.

Butler, J. 2004. *Precarious Life: The Powers of Mourning and Violence*. London: Verso.

Calhoun, C., ed. 1992. *Habermas and the Public Sphere*. Cambridge, MA: MIT Press.

Carey, J. 1989. *Communication as Culture*. Boston: Unwin Hyman.

Castells, M. 1997. *The Power of Identity*. Oxford: Blackwell.

De Certeau, M. 1984. *The Practice of Everyday Life*. Berkeley: University of California Press.

Chaney, D. 1994. *Fictions of Collective Life*. London: Sage.

Chaney, D. 2002. *Cultural Change and Everyday Life*. Basingstoke: Palgrave.

Chang, B. 1996. *Deconstructing Communication*. Minneapolis: University of Minnesota Press.

Christians, C. 1989. "Ethical Theory in a Global Setting," in T. Cooper et al., eds., *Communication Ethics and Global Change*. New York: Longman.

Christians, C. 2005. "Ethical Theory in Communications Research." *Journalism Studies* 6(1): 3–14.

Christians, C., Ferré, J., and Fackler, M. 1993. *Good News: Social Ethics and the Press*. New York: Longman.

Christians, C., Rotzoll, K., and Fackler, M. 1991. *Media Ethics: Cases and Moral Reasoning*. 3rd ed. New York: Longman.

Clifford, J. 1990. *The Predicament of Culture*. Cambridge, MA: Harvard University Press.

Cohen-Almagor, R. 2001. *Speech, Media, and Ethics: The Limits of Free Expression.* Basingstoke: Palgrave.

Cookson, R., and Jempson, M. 2004. Eds. *Satisfaction Guaranteed.* London: Mediawise.

Corlett, W. 1989. *Community without Unity: A Politics of Derridean Extravagance.* Durham, NC: Duke University Press.

Corner, J. 1995. *Television Form and Public Address.* London: Arnold.

Couldry, N. 1999. "Disrupting the Media Frame at Greenham Common: A New Chapter in the History of Mediations?" *Media, Culture, and Society* 21(3): 337–358.

Couldry, N. 2000a. *The Place of Media Power: Pilgrims and Witnesses of the Media Age.* London: Routledge.

Couldry, N. 2000b. *Inside Culture: Reimagining the Method of Cultural Studies.* London: Sage.

Couldry, N. 2000c. "Back to the Future? Rediscovering the Method in Audience Research." Talk delivered at Sussex University, February 2000.

Couldry, N. 2001a. "The Umbrella Man: Crossing a Landscape of Speech and Silence." *European Journal of Cultural Studies* 4(2): 131–152.

Couldry, N. 2001b. "A Way Out of the (Televised) Endgame?" Open Democacy, http://www.opendemoracy.net (accessed 4 October 2001).

Couldry, N. 2003a. *Media Rituals: A Critical Approach.* London: Routledge.

Couldry, N. 2003b. "Media-Meta-Capital: Extending the Range of Bourdieu's Field Theory." *Theory and Society* 32(5–6): 653–677.

Couldry, N. 2005a. "Transvaluing Media Studies: Or, Beyond the Myth of the Mediated Centre," in J. Curran and D. Morley, eds., *Media and Cultural Theory.* London: Routledge.

Couldry, N. 2005b. "The Individual Point of View: Learning from Bourdieu's Weight of the World." *Cultural Studies—Critical Methodologies* 5(3): 354–372.

Couldry, N. Forthcoming. "Media Discourse and the Naturalisation of Categories," in R. Wodak and V. Koller, eds., *Handbook of Applied Linguistics.* Amsterdam: Mouton de Gruyer.

Couldry, N., and Curran J., eds. 2003. *Contesting Media Power.* Boulder: Rowman and Littlefield.

Couldry, N., and Langer, A. 2005. "Media Consumption and Public Connection: Toward a Typology of the Dispersed Citizen." *Communication Review* 8(2): 237–258.

Couldry, N., Livingstone, S., and Markham, T. Forthcoming. *Public Connection? Media Consumption and the Presumption of Attention.* Basingstoke: Palgrave.

Crisp, R. 1996. "Modern Moral Philosophy and the Virtues," in R. Crisp, ed., *How Should One Live?* Oxford: Oxford University Press.

Croteau, D. 1995. *Politics and the Class Divide: Working People and the Middle Class Left.* Philadelphia: Temple University Press.

Curran, J. 1996. "Mass Media and Democracy Revisited," in J. Curran and M. Gurevitch, eds., *Mass Media and Society,* 2nd ed. London: Arnold.

Curran, J. 2000. "Rethinking Media and Democracy," in J. Curran and M. Gurevitch, eds., *Mass Media and Society.* 3rd ed. London: Arnold.

Curran, J. 2002. *Media and Power.* London: Routledge.

Curran, J., and Seaton, J. 2003. *Power without Responsibility.* 6th ed. London: Arnold.

Dalton, R. 2000. "Value Change and Democracy," in S. Pharr and R. Putnam, eds., *Disaffected Democracies*. Princeton, NJ: Princeton University Press.

Day, L. 2004. *Ethics in Media Communications: Cases and Controversies*. 4th ed. New York: Thomson Wadsworth.

Dayan, D., and Katz, E. 1992. *Media Events*. Cambridge, MA: Harvard University Press.

de Tocqueville, A. 1964 [1835–1840]. *Democracy in America*. London: David Campbell.

Delli Carpini, M., and Keater, S. 1996. *What Americans Know about Politics and Why It Matters*. New Haven, CT: Yale University Press.

De Man, P. 1971. *Blindness and Insight*. New Haven, CT: Yale University Press.

Delanty, G. 2003. *Community*. London: Routledge.

Derrida, J. 1997. *Politics of Friendship*. London: Verso.

Derrida, J., and Stiegler, B. 2001. *Echographies*. Cambridge: Polity.

Dewey, J. 1946 [1927]. *The Public and Its Problems*. Chicago: Gateway Books.

Downing, J. 2001. *Radical Media*, 2nd ed. Thousand Oaks, CA: Sage.

Downing, J. 2003. "Audiences and Readers of Alternative Media: The Absent Lure of the Virtually Unknown." *Media, Culture, and Society* 25(5): 625–646.

Du Gay, P., ed. 1997. *Production of Culture/Cultures of Production*. London: Sage.

Dubet, F. 1994. "The System, the Actor, and the Social Subject." *Thesis Eleven* 38: 16–35.

Dubet, F. 1995. "Sociologie du sujet et sociologie de l'expérience," in F. Dubet and M. .Wieviorcka, eds., *Penser Le Sujet*. Paris: Fayard.

Durkheim, E. 1953. "Individual and Collective Representations," in *Sociology and Philosophy*. London: Cohen and West.

Eliasoph, N. 1999. *Avoiding Politics*. Cambridge: Cambridge University Press.

Elliott, A. 2002. "The Reinvention of Citizenship," in N. Stevenson, ed., *Culture and Citizenship*. London: Sage.

Elliott, P., Murdock, G., and Schlesinger, P. 1986. "'Terrorism' and the State: A Case Study of the Discourses of Television," in R. Collins et al., eds., *Media Culture and Society: A Reader*. London: Sage.

Elshtain, J. 1997. "The Displacement of Politics," in J. Weintraub and K. Kumar, eds., *Public and Private in Thought and Practice*. Chicago: Chicago University Press.

Fabian, J. 1983. *Time and the Other*. Chicago: Chicago University Press.

Feintuck, M. 1999. *Media Regulation, Public Interest, and the Law*. Edinburgh: Edinburgh University Press.

Ferrara, A. 1998. *Reflective Authenticity*. London: Routledge.

Fiske, J. 1987. *Television Culture*. London: Methuen.

Foot, P. 2000. *Natural Goodness*. Oxford: Oxford University Press.

Foucault, M. 1977. *Language, Counter-Memory, Practice*. Ithaca, NY: Cornell University Press.

Fraser, N. 2000. "Rethinking Recognition." *New Left Review* 3: 107–120.

Freire, P. 1985. *The Politics of Education*. New York: Bergin and Garvey.

Frosh, P. 2001. "The Apocalypse Will Be Televised: A Response to Nick Couldry." Open Democracy, http://www.opendemoracy.net (accessed 24 October 2001).

Gamson, J. 1998. *Freaks Talk Back*. Chicago: Chicago University Press.

Gandy, O. 2002. "The Real Digital Divide," in L. Lievrouw and S. Livingstone, eds., *The Handbook of New Media*. London: Sage.

Ganguly, K. 2001. *States of Exception: Everyday Life and Postcolonial Identity*. Minneapolis: University of Minnesota Press.

Garnham, N. 1990. *Capitalism and Communication*. London: Sage.

Garnham, N. 1995. "Political Economy and Cultural Studies: Reconciliation or Divorce?" *Critical Studies in Mass Communication* 12(1): 62–71.

Garnham, N. 1999a. *Emancipation, the Media, and Modernity*. Oxford: Oxford University Press.

Garnham, N. 1999b. "Amartya Sen's 'Capabilities' Approach to the Evaluation of Welfare: Its Application to Communications," in A. Calabrese and J.-C. Burgelman, eds., *Communication, Citizenship, and Social Policy*. Boulder, CO: Rowman and Littlefield.

Gavin, N., ed. 1999. *The Economy, Media, and Public Knowledge*. Leicester: University of Leicester Press.

Geuss, R. 2001. *Public Goods, Private Goods*. Princeton: Princeton University Press.

Giddens, A. 1975. *The Nation-State and Violence*. Cambridge: Polity.

Giddens, A. 1984. *The Constitution of Society*. Cambridge: Polity.

Giddens, A. 1991. *Modernity and Self-Identity*. Cambridge: Polity.

Gilroy, Paul. 2000. *Between Camps*. London: Allen Lane.

Ginsburg, F. 1994. "Culture/Media: A Mild Polemic." *Anthropology Today* 10(2): 5–15.

Ginsburg, F., Abu-Lughod, J., and Larkin, B. eds. 2002. *Media Worlds*. Berkeley: University of California Press.

Giroux, H. 2003. "Youth, Higher Education, and the Crisis of Public Time: Educated Hope and the Possibility of a Democratic Future." *Social Identities* 9(2): 141–168.

Giroux, H. 2004a. *The Terror of Neoliberalism*. Boulder, CO: Paradigm Publishers.

Giroux, H. 2004b. "Public Time versus Emergency Time: Politics, Terrorism, and the Culture of Fear," in *The Abandoned Generation*. Basingstoke: Palgrave Macmillan.

Giroux, H. Forthcoming, a. "The Conservative Assault on America: Cultural Politics Education and the New Authoritarianism."

Giroux, H. Forthcoming, b. "Orwellian Newspeak and the Crisis of Politics: Representations of the Unreal in Bush's America."

Giroux, H., and Giroux, S. Searls. 2004. *Take Back Higher Education*. New York: Palgrave Macmillan.

Gitlin, T. 2001. *Media Unlimited*. New York: Henry Holt.

Gouldner, A. 1962. "'Anti-Minotaur': The Myth of a Value-Free Sociology." *Social Problems* 9: 199–213.

Glasser, T., ed. 1999. *The Idea of Public Journalism*. New York: Guilford Press.

Grindstaff, L. 2002. *The Money Shot*. Chicago: Chicago University Press.

Gripsrud, J., ed. 1999. *Television and Common Knowledge*. London: Routledge.

Gross, L., Katz, J., and Ruby, J., eds. 1988. *Image Ethics: The Moral Rights of Subjects in Photographs, Film, and Television*. Oxford University Press: New York.

Grossberg, L. 1987. "The In/difference of Television." *Screen* 28(2): 28–46.

Grossberg, L. 1992. *We Gotta Get Out of This Place*. New York: Routledge.

Grossberg, L. 1995. "Cultural Studies versus Political Economy: Is Anyone Else Bored with This Debate?" *Critical Studies in Mass Communication* 12(1): 72–81.

Habermas, J. 1989. *The Structural Transformation of the Public Sphere.* Cambridge: Polity.

Habermas, J. 1996. *Between Facts and Norms.* Cambridge: Polity.

Hall, S. 1977. "Culture, Media, and the 'Ideological Effect,'" in J. Curran et al., eds., *Mass Communications and Society.* London: Edward Arnold.

Hall, S. 1980. "Encoding/Decoding," in S. Hall, D. Hobson, A. Lowe, and P. Willis, eds., *Culture, Media, Language.* London: Unwin Hyman.

Hall, S. 1992. "What Is This 'Black' in Black Popular Culture?" in G. Dent, ed., *Black Popular Culture.* Seattle, WA: Bay Press.

Hall, S. 1997 [1987]. "Minimal Selves," in A. Gray and J. Mcguigan, eds., *Studying Culture.* London: Arnold.

Hallin, D. 1994. *We Keep America on Top of the World.* London: Routledge.

Hallin, D., and Mancini, P. 2004. *Comparing Media Systems.* Cambridge: Cambridge University Press.

Handelman, D. 1998. *Models and Mirrors.* Oxford: Berg.

Hannerz, U. 1992. *Cultural Complexity.* New York: Columbia University Press.

Hardt, H. 2005. "Communication and Power: Theory and Practice and the Aura of the Latin American Tradition." *Codigos* 1(1): 97–107.

Harrington. C., and Bielby. D. 1995. *Soap Fans.* Philadelphia: Temple University Press.

Held, D. 1995. *Democracy and the Global Order.* Cambridge: Polity.

Hermann, E., and McChesney, R. 1997. *The Global Media.* London: Cassell.

Hermes, J. 1995. *Reading Women's Magazines.* London: Sage.

Hermes, J. 1999. "Media Figures in Identity Construction," in P. Alasuutaari, ed., *Rethinking the Media Audience.* London: Sage.

Hesmondhalgh, D. 2002. *The Cultural Industries.* London: Sage.

Honneth, A. 1995. "Decentered Autonomy: The Subject after the Fall," in *The Fragmented World of the Social.* Albany, NY: SUNY Press.

hooks, b. 1994. *Teaching to Transgress: Education as the Practice of Freedom.* New York: Routledge.

Hoover, S., Schofield Clark, L. and Alters, D. 2003. *Media, Home, and Family.* London: Routledge.

Huntington, S. 1997. *The Clash of Civilisations and the Remaking of World Order.* New York: Simon and Schuster.

Hursthouse, R. 1999. *Virtue Ethics.* Oxford: Oxford University Press.

Inglehart, R. 1997. *Modernization and Postmodernization: Cultural Economic and Political Change in 43 Societies.* Princeton: Princeton University Press.

Isin, E. 2002. *Being Political: Genealogies of Citizenship.* Minneapolis: University of Minnesota Press.

Janoski, T., and Gras, B. 2002. "Political Citizenship: Foundations of Rights," in E. Isin and B. Turner, eds., *Handbook of Citizenship Studies.* London: Sage.

Jonas, H. 1984. *The Imperative of Responsibility.* Chicago: Chicago University Press.

Kaiser, J. 2003. "A Politics of Time and Space." *Tikkun* 18(6): 17–18.

Kamau, J., and Burkeman, O. 2005. "Trading Places." *Guardian,* 4 July, G2 section, pp. 1–3.

References

Kant, I. 1983 [1795]. *Perpetual Peace and Other Essays*. Indianopolis, IN: Hackett Publishing.

Kaplan, D. 2003. *Ricoeur's Critical Theory*. Albany, NY: SUNY Press.

Keane, J. 1991. *The Media and Democracy*. Cambridge: Polity.

Keane, J. 1998. *Civil Society: Old Images, New Visions*. Cambridge: Polity.

Keeble, R. 2001. *Ethics for Journalists*. London: Routledge.

Kellner, D. 2003. *Media Spectacle*. London: Routledge.

Kettle, M. 2005. "Not a War Criminal but the World's Leading Statesman." *Guardian*, 12 July, p. 22.

Kierkegaard, S. 1962 [1846-47]. *The Present Age*. London: Fontana.

Kingston, M. 2003. "Diary of a Webdiarist: Ethics Goes Online," in C. Lumby and E. Probyn, eds., *Remote Control: New Media, New Ethics*. Cambridge: Cambridge University Press.

Kitzinger, J. 1999. "A Sociology of Media Power: Key Issues in Audience Reception Research," in G. Philo, ed., *Message Received*. Harlow, UK: Longman.

Klingemann, H.-D., and Fuchs, D. 1995. *Citizens of the State*. Oxford: Oxford University Press.

Knorr-Cetina, K. 2001. "Postsocial Relations: Theorising Sociality in a Postsocial Environment," in G. Ritzer and B. Smart, eds., *The Handbook of Social Theory*. London: Sage.

Kristeva, J. 1991. *Strangers to Ourselves*. New York: Columbia University Press.

Krotz, F., and Tyler Eastman, S. 1999. "Orientations Towards Television Outside the Home." *Journal of Communication* 49 (1): 5–27.

Krugman, P. 2004. "Standard Operating Procedure." *New York Times*, 3 June, p. A17.

Kuhn, T. 1970. *The Structure of Scientific Revolutions*. 2nd ed. Chicago: Chicago University Press.

Laclau, E. 1990. "The Impossibility of Society," in *New Reflections on the Revolution of Our Time*. London: Verso.

Lambert, R. 2005. "The Path Back to Trust, Truth, and Integrity." *Guardian*, 17 January, Media section, pp. 4–5.

Lazarsfeld, P., and Merton, R. 1969 [1950]. "Mass Communication, Popular Taste and Organised Social Action," in W. Schramm, ed., *Mass Communications*, 2nd ed. Urbana: University of Illinois Press.

LeBlanc, R. 1999. *Bicycle Citizens: The Political World of the Japanese Housewife*. Berkeley: University of California Press.

Lembo, Ron 2000. *Thinking through Television*. Cambridge: Cambridge University Press.

Lemish, D. 1982. "The Rules of Viewing Television in Public Places." *Journal of Broadcasting* 26 (4): 757–782.

Levin, D. 1989. *The Listening Self*. New York: Routledge.

Lewis, J. 1991. *The Ideological Octopus*. London: Routledge.

Lewis, J. 2001. *Constructing Public Opinion*. Chicago: University of Chicago Press.

Lewis, J., Inthorn, S., and Wahl-Jorgensen, K. 2005. *Citizens or Consumers: The Media and the Decline of Political Participation*. Milton Keynes, UK: Open University Press.

Lloyd, J. 2004. *What the Media Are Doing to Our Politics*. London: Constable.

Lovibond, S. 2002. *Ethical Formation*. Cambridge, MA: Harvard University Press.

Lukes, S. 1975. "Political Ritual and Social Integration." *Sociology* 29: 289–305.

Lumby, C., and Probyn, E. 2003. "Introduction: An Ethics of Engagement," in C. Lumby and E. Probyn, eds., *Remote Control: New Media, New Ethics*. Cambridge University Press.

Maalouf, A. 2000. *On Identity*. London: Harvill Press.

Macdowell, J. 1994. *Mind and World*. Cambridge, MA: Harvard University Press.

Macdowell, J. 1998. *Mind, Value, and Reality*. Cambridge, MA: Harvard University Press.

MacIntyre, A. 1981. *After Virtue*. London: Duckworth.

MacIntyre, A. 1999. *Dependent Rational Animals*. London: Duckworth.

Marcos, Subcomandante. 2000. "Le fascisme libéral." *Le monde diplomatique*, August 1, pp. 14–15.

Mann, M. 1970. "The Social Cohesion of Liberal Democracy." *American Sociological Review* 35(3): 423–439.

Marcus, George 1999. "The Use of Complicity in the Changing Mise-en-scène of Anthropological Fieldwork," in S. Ortner, ed., *The Fate of "Culture."* Berkeley: University of California Press.

Marshall, T. 1992. "Citizenship and Social Class ," in T. Marshall and T. Bottomore. London: Pluto.

Martin-Barbero, J. 1993. *Communication, Culture, and Hegemony*. London: Sage.

Martuccelli, D. 2002. *Grammaires de l'Individu*. Paris: Seuil.

Mattelart, A., Delcourt, X., and Mattelart, M. 1984. *International Image Markets*. London: Comedia.

Mattelart, M., and Mattelart, A. 1990. *The Carnival of Images: Brazilian Television Fiction*. New York: Bergin and Garvey.

Mayhew, L. 1997. *The New Public*. Cambridge: Cambridge University Press.

McCarthy, A. 2002. *Ambient Television: Visual Culture and Public Space*. Durham, NC: Duke University Press.

McNay, L. 1999. "Gender, Habitus, and Field: Pierre Bourdieu and the Limits of Reflexivity." *Theory, Culture, and Society* 16(1): 95–117.

McQuail, D. 1987. *Mass Communication Theory: An Introduction*. 2nd ed. London: Sage.

Mead, G. 1967 [1934]. *Mind, Self, and Society*. Chicago: Chicago University Press.

Melucci, A. 1996. *Challenging Codes*. Cambridge: Cambridge University Press.

Meyer, T. 2003. *Media Democracy*. Cambridge: Polity.

Meyrowitz, J. 1994. "Medium Theory," in D. Crowley and D. Mitchell, eds., *Communication Theory Today*. Cambridge: Polity.

Mill, J. S. 1929 [1859]. *On Liberty*. London: Watts.

Mills, C. Wright. 1956. *The Power Elite*. Oxford: Oxford University Press.

Mills, C. Wright. 1970 [1959]. *The Sociological Imagination*. Harmondsworth: Penguin.

Morley, D. 1980. "Texts, Readers, Subjects," in S. Hall, D. Hobson, A. Lowe, and P. Willis, eds.. *Culture, Media, Language*. London: Unwin Hyman.

Morley, D. 1986. *Family Television*. London: BFI.

Morley, D. 1992. *Television, Audiences, and Cultural Studies*. London: Routledge.

Mouffe, C. 2000. *The Democratic Paradox*. London: Verso.

Mueller, M. 2004. "Reinventing Media Activism: Public Interest Advocacy in the Making of U.S. Communication-Information Policy," available from www.digital-convergence.org/ (accessed July 2004).

Murdock, G. 2000. "Reconstructing the Ruined Tower: Contemporary Communications and Questions of Class," in J. Curran and M. Gurevitch, eds., *Mass Media and Society*, 3rd ed. London: Arnold.

Nancy, J.-L. 1991. *The Inoperative Community*. Minneapolis: University of Minnesota Press.

Norris, C. 1987. *Derrida*. London: Fontana.

Nussbaum, M. 1993. "Non-Relative Virtues: An Aristotelian Approach," in M. Nussbaum and A. Sen, eds., *The Quality of Life*. Oxford: Oxford University Press.

O'Connor, A. 2005. *Raymond Williams*. Lanham, MD: Rowman and Littlefield.

O'Leary, B. 2001. "The Right to Rights." Open Democracy, http://www.opendemoracy.net (accessed 18 September 2001).

O'Neill, J. 1992. "Journalism in the Marketplace," in A. Belsey, and R. Chadwick, eds., *Ethical Issues in Journalism and the Media*. London: Routledge.

O'Neill, O. 1990. "Practices of Toleration," in J. Lichtenberg, ed., *Democracy and the Mass Media*. Cambridge: Cambridge University Press.

O'Neill, O. 1996. *Towards Justice and Virtue*. Cambridge: Cambridge University Press.

O'Neill, O. 2000. "Distant Strangers, Moral Standing and Porous Boundaries," in *Bounds of Justice*. Cambridge: Cambridge University Press.

O'Neill, O. 2002. *A Question of Trust*. Cambridge: Cambridge University Press.

O'Neill, O. 2005. "Speaking and Deceiving." Lecture delivered at London School of Economics, 1 February.

Oakley, J., and Cocking, D. 2001. *Virtue Ethics and Professional Roles*. Cambridge: Cambridge University Press.

Pateman, C. 1970. *Participation and Democratic Theory*. Cambridge: Cambridge University Press.

Pettit, P. 1999. *Republicanism*. Oxford: Oxford University Press.

Press, Andrea. 1991. *Women Watching Television*. Philadelphia: University of Pennsylvania Press.

Pritchard, D. 2000. "The Future of Media Accountability," in D. Pritchard, ed., *Holding the Media Accountable: Citizens, Ethics, and the Law*. Indiana: Indiana University Press.

Quinn, W. 1995. "Putting Rationality in Its Place," in R. Hursthouse, G. Lawrence, and W. Quinn, eds., *Virtues and Reasons: Philippa Foot and Moral Theory*. Oxford: Oxford University Press.

Radway, J. 1988. "Reception Study: Ethnography and the Problem of the Dispersed Audience and Nomadic Subjects." *Cultural Studies* 2(3): 359–376.

Rappaport, R. 1999. *Ritual and Religion in the Making of Humanity*. Cambridge: Cambridge University Press.

Rawls, J. 1972. *A Theory of Justice*. Oxford: Oxford University Press.

Rawls, J. 1996. *Political Liberalism*. Cambridge: Cambridge University Press.

Reckwitz, A. 2002. "Toward a Theory of Social Practices." *European Journal of Social Theory* 5(2): 243–263.

Ricoeur, P. 1992. *Oneself as Another*. Chicago: Chicago University Press.

Ricoeur, P. 1995. "Reflections on a New Ethos for Europe." *Philosophy and Social Criticism*, 21(5/6).

Rifkin, J. 2001. "Quand les marchés s'effacent devant les reseaux." *Le Monde Diplomatique*, July 2001, pp. 22–23.

Robins, K. 1995. *Into the Image*. London: Routledge.

Rodriguez, C. 2001. *Fissures in the Mediascape*. Creskill, NJ: Hampton Press.

Rodriguez, C. 2003. "The Bishop and His Star: Citizens' Communication in Southern Chile," in N. Couldry and J. Curran, eds., *Contesting Media Power*. Lanham, MD: Rowman and Littlefield.

Rorty, R. 1979. *Philosophy and the Mirror of Nature*. Princeton: Princeton University Press.

Rose, N. 1996. "The Death of the Social? Re-figuring the Territory of Government." *Economy and Society* 25(3): 327–356.

Rousseau, J.-J. 1968. *Politics and the Arts*. Ithaca, NY: Cornell University Press.

Rousseau, J.-J. 1973. "The Social Contract," in *The Social Contract and Discourses*. London: Everyman Library.

Sassen, S. 2001. "A Message from the Global South." *Guardian*, 12 September, p. 23.

Sassen, S. 2002. "Towards Post-National and Denationalised Citizenship," in E. Isin and B. Turner, eds., *Handbook of Citizenship Studies*. London: Sage.

Sattuc, D. 2004. *Darkness at Dawn*. New Haven, CT: Yale University Press.

Scannell, P. 1996. *Radio, Television, and Modern Life*. Oxford: Blackwell.

Scannell, P. 1988. "Radio Times: The Temporal Arrangements of Broadcasting in the Modern World," in P. Drummond and R. Paterson, eds., *Television and Its Audiences*. London: BFI.

Schatzki, T. 1999. *Social Practices: A Wittgensteinian Approach to Human Activity and the Social*. Cambridge: Cambridge University Press.

Schiller, H. 1969. *Mass Communications and American Empire*. Boulder, CO: Westview Press.

Schroder, K. 2000. "Making Sense of Audience Discourses." *European Journal of Cultural Studies* 3(2): 233–258.

Seiter, E. 1999. *New Media Audiences*. Oxford: Oxford University Press.

Sen, A. 1992. *Inequality Reexamined*. Oxford: Oxford University Press.

Sen, A. 1999. *Development as Freedom*. Oxford: Oxford University Press.

Sennett, R. 2003. *Respect*. Penguin: Harmondsworth.

Sennett, R., and Cobb, J. 1972. *The Hidden Injuries of Class*. Cambridge: Cambridge University Press.

Shabi, R 2005. "The War on Dissent." *Guardian*, 2 July, p. 20.

Shils, E. 1975. *Center and Periphery*. Chicago: Chicago University Press.

Signorielli, N., and Morgan, D., eds. 1990. *Cultivation Analysis: New Directions in Media Effects Research*. Newbury Park: Sage.

Silk, M. 2003. "Islam and the American News Media Post–September 11," in D. Mitchell and S. Marriage, eds., *Mediating Religion*. London: T and T Clark.

Silverstone, R. 1994. *Television and Everyday Life*. London: Routledge.

Silverstone, R. 2003. "Proper Distance: Towards an Ethics of Cyberspace," in G. Listol, A. Morrison, and T. Rasmussen, eds., *Digital Media Revisited*. Cambridge, MA: MIT Press.

Silverstone, R. Forthcoming, a. *Morality and Media*. Cambridge: Polity.

References

Silverstone, R. Forthcoming, b. "Media and Communication," in C. Calhoun, C. Rojek, and B. Turner, eds., *The Handbook of Sociology*. London: Sage.

Silverstone, R., and Hirsch, E., eds. 1992. *Consuming Technologies*. London: Routledge.

Sinclair, J., Jacka, E. and Cunningham, S. 1996. *New Patterns in Global Television*. Oxford: Oxford University Press.

Sinha, D. 2004. "Religious Fundamentalism and Its 'Other': A Snapshot View from the Global Information Order," in S. Saha, ed. *Religious Fundamentalism in the Contemporary World*. Lanham, MD: Lexington Books.

Slote, M. 2001. *Morals from Motives*. Oxford: Oxford University Press.

Smith, D. 1987. *The Everyday World as Problematic: A Feminist Sociology*. Boston: Northwestern Press.

Spivak, G. 1990. *The Postcolonial Critic*. New York: Routledge.

Stiegler, B. 2004. *Mécréance et discrédit*. Paris: Galilée.

Stevenson, N. 2002. "Culture and Citizenship: An Introduction," in N. Stevenson, ed., *Culture and Citizenship*. London: Sage.

Sunstein, C. 1993. *Democracy and the Problem of Free Speech*. New York: Free Press.

Sunstein, C. 2000. *Republic.com*. Princeton: Princeton University Press.

Swidler, A. 2001. "What Anchors Cultural Practices," in T. Schatzki, K. Knorr Cetina, and E. von Savigny, eds., *The Practice Turn in Contemporary Theory*. London: Routledge.

Tanaka, G. 2003. *The Intercultural Campus*. New York: Peter Lang.

Tarde, G. 1969 [1922]. *Communication and Social Opinion*. Chicago: Chicago University Press.

Taylor, C. 1986. "Foucault on Freedom and Truth," in *Philosophy and the Human Sciences: Philosophical Papers*, vol. 2. Cambridge: Cambridge University Press.

Taylor, C. 1994. *Multiculturalism*. Ed. Amy Gutman. Princeton: Princeton University Press.

Thompson, M. 1995. "The Representation of Life," in R. Hursthouse, G. Lawrence, and W. Quinn, eds., *Virtues and Reasons: Philippa Foot and Moral Theory*. Oxford: Oxford University Press.

Tomlinson, J. 1991. *Cultural Imperialism*. London: Pinter.

Touraine, A. 1988. *Return of the Actor*. Minneapolis: University of Minnesota Press.

Touraine, A. 2000. *Can We Live Together?* Cambridge: Polity.

Tulloch, J. 2000. *Watching Television Audiences*. London: Arnold.

Tully, J. 1995. *Strange Multiplicity: Constitutionalism in an Age of Diversity*. Cambridge: Cambridge University Press.

Turner, B. 2001. "The Erosion of Citizenship." *British Journal of Sociology* 52(2): 189–209.

Turner, B. 2002. "Outline of a General Theory of Citizenship," in N. Stevenson, ed., *Culture and Citizenship*. London: Sage.

Turner, G. 2003. "Ethics, Entertainment, and the Tabloid: The Case of Talkback Radio in Australia," in C. Lumby and E. Probyn, eds., *Remote Control: New Media, New Ethics*. Cambridge: Cambridge University Press.

Turner, G., Bonner, F., and Marshall, D. 2000. *Fame Games*. Cambridge: Cambridge University Press.

References

Turner, V. 1974. *Dramas: Fields and Metaphors.* Cornell: Cornell University Press.

Urry, J. 2000. *Sociology Beyond Societies.* London: Sage.

Wacquant, L. 2002. "From Slavery to Mass Incarceration: Rethinking the 'Race Question' in the United States." *New Left Review* 13: 41–60.

Walter, T. 1999. "The Questions People Asked," in T. Walter, ed., *Mourning for Diana.* Oxford: Berg.

Wark, M. 1999. *Celebrities, Culture, and Cyberspace.* Sydney: Pluto.

Warner, Michael. 2002. *Publics and Counter-Publics.* New York: Zone Books.

Weber, M. 1947. *The Theory of Social and Economic Organisation.* New York: Free Press.

Weber, M. 1991a. "The Sociology of Charismatic Authority," in H. Gerth and C. Wright Mills, eds., *From Max Weber.* London: Routledge.

Weber, M. 1991b. "Science as a Vocation," in H. Gerth and C. Wright Mills, eds., *From Max Weber.* London: Routledge.

Weintraub, J., and Kumar, K., eds., 1997. *Public and Private in Thought and Practice.* Chicago: Chicago University Press.

West, C. 1993. *Keeping Faith: Philosophy and Race in America.* London: Routledge.

White, R. 2003. "The Emerging 'Communitarian' Ethics of Public Communication," in J. Mitchell and S. Marriage, eds., *Mediating Religion.* London: T and T Clarke.

Williams, B. 1985. *Ethics and the Limits of Philosophy.* London: Fontana/Collins.

Williams, B. 2002. *Truth and Truthfulness: An Essay in Genealogy.* Princeton: Princeton University Press.

Williams, R. 1958. *Culture and Society: 1780–1950.* Harmondsworth: Penguin.

Williams, R. 1961. *The Long Revolution.* Harmondsworth: Penguin.

Williams, R. 1968. *Communications.* 2nd ed. Harmondsworth: Penguin.

Williams, R. 1993 [1961]. "Letter to WEA Tutors," in J. McIlroy and S. Westwood, eds., *Border Country: Raymond Williams in Adult Education.* Leicester: National Institute of Adult Continuing Education.

Williams, R. 2005. "The Media: Public Interest and Common Good," full text of Archbishop speech given June 15, available from http://www.guardian.co.uk/religion/story/0,2763,1507300,00.html.

Wolin, S. 1992. "What Revolutionary Action Means Today," in C. Mouffe, ed., *Dimensions of Radical Democracy.* London: Verso.

Wolin, S. 1996. "Fugitive Democracy," in S. Benhabib, ed., *Democracy and Difference.* Princeton, NJ: Princeton University Press.

Wright, H. 1998. "Dare We Decentre Birmingham? Troubling the 'Origin' and Trajectories of Cultural Studies." *European Journal of Cultural Studies* 1(1): 33–56.

Wrong, D. 1994. *The Problem of Order.* New York: Free Press.

Young, I. M. 2000. *Inclusion and Democracy.* Oxford: Oxford University Press.

Younge, G. 2005. "Blair's Blowback." *Guardian,* 11 July, p. 21.

Zelizer, B. 1993. *Covering the Body.* Chicago: Chicago University Press.

Zolo, D. 1992. *Democracy and Complexity.* Cambridge: Cambridge University Press.

Index

✤

Index

Ferrara, Alessandro, 67
Film: culture of, 29; distribution, 88
First Amendment (U.S. Constitution), 106, 108, 123
First nature, 116
Fiske, John, 24
Foot, Philippa, 115, 117, 118
Foucault, Michel, 47, 48, 82n, 144n
Fragmentation, 69–70, 79
Fraser, Nancy, 91
Freedom, 4, 85, 141
Free market, media and, 104, 120
Free media, 101, 134; deception and, 136
Freire, Paulo, 57, 141
Functionalism, 16–17, 18, 22, 41–42

Gandy, Oscar: on personalization, 78
Garnham, Nicholas, 26, 121, 122
G-8 Gleneagles Summit, 19, 20, 21, 31n, 72
General Council of the Press, 105
General Medical Council, 105
Geographical area, community and, 64
Giddens, 14; structuration theory and, 42
GIO. *See* Global Information Order
Giroux, Henry, 71, 76, 81n
Glasgow Media Group, 25, 26
Global dialogue, 107, 117
Global Information Order (GIO), 88, 89, 98, 99, 100
Globalization, 65, 94, 99
Good, questions of, 115
Government, process of, 135
Gras, Brian, 65
Greenham Common U.S. Air Force Base, protest at, 71
Grossberg, Larry, 26, 39, 73
Guardian, 99; language of, 20; on September 11, 98
Guattari, conceptual explorations of, 41

Habermas, Jurgen, 78, 108; public sphere and, 29, 109
Hall, Stuart, 55
Handelman, Don, 17
Hardt, Hanno, 7, 8
Harm: avoiding, 120–122, 132–133; institutions and, 132, 134
Hatred, media and, 131
Haw, Brian, 71, 72
Hearing, vision and, 6
Hegemony, struggles for, 90

Heidegger, Martin, 41
Herman, Barbara, 143n
Hesmondhalgh, Dave, 81n
Honneth, Alex, 67
Houses of Parliament, protest at, 71
Human excellence, media and, 125
Human functionings, 121, 122
Human rights, politics and, 64
Human space, remoralization of, 66
Huntington, Samuel, 94
Hursthouse, Rosalind, 124
Hutchins Commission, 106
Huxley, Aldous, 71

Identity, 2, 24, 42, 46; collective, 68; construction, 38; difference and, 58; expressing, 75; politics, 74; public performance of, 40
Image, 96, 100n; ethics of, 98, 145n; word and, 97–100
Incorporation/resistance paradigm, 37
Independent, on London bombings, 98–99
Individual, social underpinnings of, 24
Individualization, 14, 65, 78
Inequalities, 73; influence of, 94, 95, 96; power, 86, 142n; reduction of, 97
Information, 119, 133; accurate, 124; concentration of, 92; ethics of, 7; flows, 13, 96; online, 27; seeking, 43; socially relevant, 125; sources of, 26
Injustice, 89–92
Inoperative community, theory of, 66, 78
Inside Culture (Couldry), 54, 69
Institutions, 14, 25, 87, 125, 145n; accountability for, 101; ethics and, 101–102, 130; freedoms of, 135; funding for, 136; harms by, 132; harms to, 134; individuals and, 127; interests of, 127–128; nonmedia, 135–137; trust in, 128–129; understanding of, 2
Instrumental rationality, value and, 87
International Communication Association (ICA), 143n
International relations, September 11 and, 86
Iraq: September 11 and, 19; war in, 19, 21, 61
Isin, Engin, 71

Janoski, Thomas, 65
Jerry Springer Show, 44

About the Author

⌁

Nick Couldry is Reader in Media, Communications, and Culture at the London School of Economics and Political Science. He is the author or editor of five books including *Media Rituals: A Critical Approach* (Routledge 2003), *The Place of Media Power* (Routledge 2000), and (coedited with James Curran) *Contesting Media Power* (Rowman and Littlefield 2003).